CW01237436

Theorizing War

Also by Nick Mansfield

MASOCHISM: The Art of Power

CULTURAL STUDIES AND THE NEW HUMANITIES (*with Patrick Fuery*)

SUBJECTIVITY: Theories of the Self from Freud to Haraway

CULTURAL STUDIES AND CRITICAL THEORY (*with Patrick Fuery*)

Theorizing War

From Hobbes to Badiou

Nick Mansfield

palgrave
macmillan

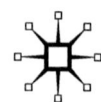

© Nick Mansfield 2008.

All rights reserved. No reproduction, copy or transmission of this publication may be made without written permission.

No portion of this publication may be reproduced, copied or transmitted save with written permission or in accordance with the provisions of the Copyright, Designs and Patents Act 1988, or under the terms of any licence permitting limited copying issued by the Copyright Licensing Agency, Saffron House, 6-10 Kirby Street, London EC1N 8TS.

Any person who does any unauthorized act in relation to this publication may be liable to criminal prosecution and civil claims for damages.

The author has asserted his right to be identified as the author of this work in accordance with the Copyright, Designs and Patents Act 1988.

First published 2008 by
PALGRAVE MACMILLAN

Palgrave Macmillan in the UK is an imprint of Macmillan Publishers Limited, registered in England, company number 785998, of Houndmills, Basingstoke, Hampshire RG21 6XS.

Palgrave Macmillan in the US is a division of St Martin's Press LLC, 175 Fifth Avenue, New York, NY 10010.

Palgrave Macmillan is the global academic imprint of the above companies and has companies and representatives throughout the world.

Palgrave® and Macmillan® are registered trademarks in the United States, the United Kingdom, Europe and other countries.

ISBN-13: 978–0–230–53732–3 hardback
ISBN-10: 0–230–53732–4 hardback

This book is printed on paper suitable for recycling and made from fully managed and sustained forest sources. Logging, pulping and manufacturing processes are expected to conform to the environmental regulations of the country of origin.

A catalogue record for this book is available from the British Library.

Library of Congress Cataloging-in-Publication Data
Mansfield, Nick.
  Theorizing war : from Hobbes to Badiou / Nick Mansfield.
    p. cm.
  Includes bibliographical references (p.).
  ISBN 978–0–230–53732–3
  1. War (Philosophy) I. Title.
  B105. W3M37 2008
  355.0201—dc22   2008021217

10	9	8	7	6	5	4	3	2	1
17	16	15	14	13	12	11	10	09	08

Printed and bound in Great Britain by
CPI Antony Rowe, Chippenham and Eastbourne

To my brothers, Martin and Paul

Contents

Acknowledgments	viii
Introduction: War and Its Other	1
Part I Posing the Problem	9
Hobbes: War redeemed by sovereignty	9
Kant: Peace through war	19
Clausewitz: War as the activation of the social	28
Part II The War/Other Complex	39
Freud: War and ambivalence	40
Bataille: War, consumption and religion	63
Deleuze and Guattari: Owning the war-machine	82
Under the black light: Derrida, Levinas, Schmitt and the aporia of war	98
Part III The Problem of Difference	119
The collapse of difference: Insisting on Clausewitz	119
Global war	141
Recovering difference	150
Conclusion: War and Human Rights	162
Bibliography	169
Index	172

Acknowledgments

Parts of this book were originally published as "Under the Black Light: Derrida, War and Human Rights" in *Mosaic*, 40 (2), 2007, 151–64, and as "War and Its Other: Between Bataille and Derrida" in *Theory and Event*, 9/4, 2006.

Thanks to everyone who has put up with me going on about war in recent years, and above all, thanks to the usual suspects: Bonny, Oskar and Tilde, without whom nothing would be much good.

Introduction: War and Its Other

In *Philosophy in a Time of Terror*, in a discussion of the opposition between "war" and "terrorism," Jacques Derrida tells Giovanna Borradori that the terms themselves are unstable and have a political history that must be rigorously examined:

> Semantic instability, irreducible trouble spots on the borders between concepts, indecision in the very concept of the border: all this must not only be analysed as a speculative disorder, a conceptual chaos or zone of passing turbulence in public or political language. We must also recognise here strategies and relations of force. The dominant power is the one that manages to impose and, thus, to legitimate, indeed to legalise (for it is always a question of law) on a national or world stage, the terminology and thus the interpretation that best suits it in a given situation.
>
> (Borradori, 2003, p. 105)

He cites two examples of how the terms "war" and "terrorism" have been manipulated in historical circumstances in order to fulfil certain political goals. One is the retrospective definition by the French parliament in the 1990s of the Algerian War as an international war, and not a domestic conflict, so veterans would have access to certain classes of military entitlements (p. 104); the other, the insistence of the US government that any resistance to the established governments of South America be denoted as terrorism (p. 105).

We all think we know what war is, but the term "war" has a history and cannot simply be taken for granted. Certain legal thresholds have to be crossed for collective violence to be officially recognised as war. Since the Treaty of Westphalia, the most common way of understanding this is that war is the prerogative of states, or at least of political organisations that aspire to be states. Yet, Derrida's comments remind us that, even allowing for these legal constraints, war itself is not a simple thing to identify, and is not always identified. The term may pre- or post-date certain events that may, at the time, be experienced and represented completely differently. War's meaning is unstable and problematic, and the use of the term is more than just a simple act of description. Indeed, the term "war" can only be applied once certain other conditions are in place. Not least of these conditions is that war must always emerge in relation to other ideas, terms and concepts, and is always in relation to them, even if these are not always explicitly articulated. The aim of this book is to show that the deployment of the term "war" is inevitably a deployment of something else as well, the "other" of war, something called variously peace, or civil society, or sovereign authority, or love or friendship. Yet, this other is not a simple opposite to war, something that we aim to protect from war or retrieve from it somehow. The deployment of the term "war" is made possible only by the deployment of this other term. It is indeed, often, perhaps usually, the deployment of this other to war that licenses war and makes it possible.

The term "war" is not then a simple descriptor of an unambiguous fact or a naturally occurring phenomenon. Governments sometimes hesitate to apply the term to their own aggressive military activity. Since the Second World War, the declaration of war has declined in importance. This may be because governments may want to allow certain impressions about their activities to endure: that they are merely supporting—even just "advising"—an ally, or targeting a rogue organisation with no real political standing, in a brief police action. Military activity, here, is seen as almost medicinal, a short sharp cure, a course of therapy for low functioning nation states, or the quarantining of an unpredictable political contagion. These activities do not quite cross the threshold to become real "war," and so the term itself is not activated officially, and emerges only as the shorthand excitement—or incitement—of journalists. On the other hand, as has been widely observed, governments can all too quickly denote as war things traditionally seen as the domain of social policy. Social problems as mundane as substance abuse, crime and poverty are now dealt with by wars. The declaration of war has become a regular and random re-announcement that deviant social practices, and inevitably deviant social groups, are present within the social field, and must be annihilated. Governments do not declare war on one another anymore, even as they send their children out to fight, but societies do declare undefined and potentially interminable wars on fractions of themselves. Of course, the "war on terror" transposes this kind of indefinite war onto the body of the earth itself.

So, we have wars that do not apparently deserve the name, and non-wars that do. The use of the term then is more than the identification of a specific type of well-known event. It is the recognition of a complex state of affairs in which the relationships between, and even the nature of, governments, social relationships, ideals and affects are all in play. To not call violent state military action "war" is to refuse to recognise your antagonist as in any way in a symmetrical relationship with you. This claims a certain status for you and your values that it refuses to concede to your enemy. It is an instant statement about your own social meaning and your enemy's. To call your own society's ordinary internal dynamics "war" is to apply a certain measure of exclusion to those living within your polis, disenfranchising them as superfluous to social meaning. The use of the term "war" then is the enactment of a certain idea of what society is or should be, and how that vision might possibly be achieved. Both of these instances of the use and non-use of the term are enactments of developed and complicated views of those things that are not war. It is in the deployment of these understandings of war in terms of what is the other to it that the meaning and planning of war is produced. War is always seen as a reflection of what human society is like, from the communal to the global, or as the means to change it to attain some particular goal. War makes sense only in relation to what is the other to it. The other of war marks the limits of warfare and that thing that war must always refer to in order to make any sense at all. It is the aim of this book to investigate war in the light of this otherness. What are the others that trigger and legitimise war, how does this relationship work and what does it reveal about us?

The question becomes therefore not what the term "war" denotes, but how it emerges as meaningful in relation to other meanings which are themselves emerging, or are already extant. These other meanings range from concepts in political theory through historical events to aesthetic speculation and the enactment of individual subjectivity. From rigorous idea to casual contrivance, from enduring ideology to passing feeling, from the social to the personal and the institutional to the makeshift, the others of war derive from multiple and intersecting fields, as well as from different, perhaps even incommensurate intellectual domains. We will see the other of war as determined by various discourses ranging from the political thinking of Hobbes, Kant, Schmitt and Mbembe to military theory in Clausewitz, the analysis of individual and collective subjectivity in Freud and Žižek, history in Foucault, religion in Bataille, the media in Baudrillard, philosophy in Derrida and Badiou, activism in Hardt and Negri, urban planning in Virilio, speculation in Deleuze and Guattari, and sociology in Bauman and Hirst. We can apply no single disciplinary measure to this range of thinkers, nor can we see them as the full population of a discrete and knowable domain with inherited limits. They have been chosen not because they are the canonical thinkers of war, nor because they represent a complete list. Some readers will be surprised to know how much some of the writers included here have actually had to say on the subject, and how original it has been. They have been chosen in order to allow to emerge a sense of the issues at stake in an account of what war is in theory, and because they present a range of thinkers of war's relationship to its other that will allow us to define that particular complex and the discussion that focuses on it. I believe it is only by unravelling this particular complex that the problem of war can be dealt with. This book then organises various writings into a structure that gives a shape to the undeclared debates between various positions, while at the same time treating each text in its distinctiveness to allow to appear the untidiness, disproportion and variations in emphasis that different writers working in different disciplines bring to the one topic. There is a convergence between different positions but no homogeneity.

Yet a clear trajectory emerges. The first section of this book aims to pose the problem of war's relationship with its other. In both Hobbes and Kant, war is seen as the thing that human beings institute civil society and sovereign authority in order to escape. War here is in direct contradiction with organised and legitimate sociality. In Clausewitz, on the other hand, war is an enactment of political intention and, indeed in the end, of the social body conceived as a totality. Here the problem is posed: Is war the opposite of its other or an extension of it? If here the other of war is civil society, then is war in contradiction with society, or continuous with it? Are they opposites or the same?

In the second section, we look at thinkers of war who have tried to deal directly with this problem. How can war be both an enactment of an individual society's intentions and at the same time the thing that most undermines, contradicts and perhaps even ruins the various principles on which sociality depends? How can it be both that which fulfils society's purposes and that which most threatens them? In Freud, this complex is understood as an enactment of the ambivalence of all relationships, indeed all psychological states. Repression is required to ensure the civility of functioning social relations. Yet, this inevitably produces a reaction where "primitive" emotion is constrained and intensified, eventually seeking to break out in explosions of violence. The pressure that facilitates workable social relations produces the counter-action that most threatens them. In Bataille, warfare is linked to the extravagant festivals wherein societies temporarily break the hold the rational logic of the workaday world has on them, and indulge in the world of luxury, extravagance and destructiveness. The military order, which attempts to harness the violent energy of war to society's rational programmes, lives a contradiction then by attempting to combine a logic of meaningful purpose with the exultant chaos of primal violence. In Deleuze and Guattari, this ambivalence is lived out in the relationship between the order of civil society and the "war-machines" either internal to it or that it attempts to appropriate for its own purposes. Finally, Derrida deconstructs the binary oppositions on which the meaning of war depends: between war and peace, on the one hand, and between friend and enemy, on the other. The result is a conception of war emerging in a field of shifting and intersecting identities in multiple and mobile relationship with one another.

In the third section, we look at a range of recent and contemporary discussions of war, which, taken as a whole, converge on the idea that the difference between war and civil society, or war and peace, has been lost. This has become the most common account of the relationship between war and its other in recent times. Sometimes it is asserted provocatively; sometimes argued in a subtle, complex and nuanced way. However it is presented, it represents the view of war and its relationship with its other that we most need to consider in our time. It returns to some of the issues outlined above: we live in an era where wars are undeclared and disguise themselves as police actions, while the police are quite happy to declare themselves to be at war on the streets of our cities. War becomes regular and ubiquitous. We do not really have peace anymore and war itself is everywhere. It is mundane and continuous, yet seamlessly co-ordinated with social life. There seems to be a convergence between war and its other, a disappearance of the difference between them. It has become therefore a cliché of contemporary commentary to say that war and peace have increasingly come to converge on one another, perhaps even to become indistinguishable. Derrida, himself, has made such a statement, when he claims that it is techno-science that has made the increasing indifference between war and peace possible (Borradori, 2003, p. 101). Often, this non-distinction is seen as the triumph of the war party, or the complete militarisation of society. At other times, it is seen as a mere illustration of Clausewitz's argument about the co-ordination of war and policy. Both of these views have been intensely seductive to recent commentators, partly because they seem to account for the shifting and increasingly complicated and plural relationship between war and the social, sometimes simply for the vituperative critical energy that loads the association.

My aim is to contest the view that there has been a loss of difference between war and peace, and the associated view that only by restoring this difference can we make peace really available. I aim to show that the difference between war and its other is not something that we should energise, the distinction on which our hope of perpetual peace rests, but the difference that makes war potentially meaningful and that is constantly referred to by politicians in their rationalisations of aggressive policy. In other words, the distinction between war and its other is very much alive, and our attempts to recover its strictness are not necessarily a way of making peace possible, but of making war perpetually available.

Some more complex way of understanding the relationship between war and its other is necessary, one in which the ineluctable interpenetration of the two can be known. The version of the war/other double most at stake at present is the rivalry between war and human rights discourse. Wars fought across the globe render democracy an increasingly remote dream for whole societies. On the Home Front, civil rights are increasingly seen as a luxury. These wars are opposed vehemently by the constant re-assertion of the irreducibility of human rights. Yet, it is these very human rights that are announced as the justification of the war in the first place. We are fighting for liberty, democracy, the enfranchisement of women and so on. Of course, a nation's motives for going to war are never uncomplicated or un-mixed. Economics, strategic advantage, prestige and revenge may all play their part, along with a thousand other inspirations. Yet, it is too easy to simply dismiss professed concerns for human rights as mere pretence. Human rights cause wars, "just" and "righteous" wars, which are justified by politico-media gestures like the Blair doctrine. Who amongst us does not believe some violence is justified in the name of human rights? Who has not been frustrated that democratic governments have not done more—including military violence—to intervene in states that use rape, torture, imprisonment, occupation, corporal punishment, ethnic brutality, over-policing, military intimidation and so on to preserve the rule of race-based, military, theocratic or mere gangster governments? Who, in short, does not believe that there is a role for violence in the advancement of civility? War is simultaneously contradicted and incited by the discourse of human rights. It is not possible, therefore, to simply see the highest standards of political value and war as mere opposites. Nor, however, can we deny that war will always threaten human rights in the theatres in which it is played out, and at home. This complex does not make the challenge of negotiating our way through war easy. Without this irreducible difference between war and what justifies it, war would not exist. Without the others that refute it, and that it claims to love and defend, there would be no war. It is in the hope of contributing somehow to the simplification of this problem in a way that will make truly political decisions, and not mere academic analysis, possible that this book has been written.

Part I
Posing the Problem

One of the two most influential accounts of the relationship between war and its other sees war and civil society as opposites. Here, legal authority has been constituted in order to save humanity from its natural state, which is one of a violent competition understood as war. The second account sees war as a continuation, even implementation, of social purposes and values. The first is associated most famously with Thomas Hobbes, and the second with Carl von Clausewitz. These two rival accounts map out the poles of our discussion of the relationship between war and its other: Are war and its other in contradiction or continuous with one another? Later, we will see a range of accounts that attempt to combine the two, arguing for a complex and dynamic relationship where the two simultaneously incite and defy one another. In this chapter, we will present these two as distinct alternatives in order to provide some basic reference point which will connect our discussion with the most common ways of thinking about war. In popular discourse, commentators often simply assume unthinkingly either Hobbes's or Clausewitz's position, or both, even in the one argument. Despite their continuing popularity, however, they only go a limited way towards understanding the complexity of our relationship with war. In fact, as we shall see, these thinkers actually evince far more complicated and unstable positions than they are usually given credit for.

Hobbes: War redeemed by sovereignty

War shames us. No longer the hygiene of nations, war is something to be avoided or overcome. We dream of its final annihilation, even while we look to violence for entertainment, hope someone's army will topple someone else's despot, and pumped up by adrenaline, peer agonisingly into the labyrinthine landscapes of violent computer games. War is the opposite of what we want, even though we pay for it, vote for it, and trust in it. Our word for peace is security, the confession that the only quiet we know is perpetually armed and prepared to be ruthless. In short, our actions might say otherwise, but we like to understand war and peace as opposites to one another. The aim of this section is to discuss the most influential formulation of the idea that war and peace are diametrically opposite. Thomas Hobbes provided an account in which this opposition defined social relations. According to this argument, it was in order to control war, the natural human impulse to violence, that sovereign political authority as the lodestone of civil society was instituted in the first place. Yet, as we will see, what this means is that war continuously haunts society and politics as the underside that they can never quite succeed in abandoning.

Hobbes's account of the formation of civil society as the institution of sovereign power implies a narrative in two phases: human beings in their natural state are pitted in competition with one another, because in nature the only purpose and logic they can pursue is self-interest and self-protection. Inevitably, they realise that the chaos this produces is, in fact, in no one's interest. These "natural" goals cannot be achieved in nature, a place where there is only disorder. Everyone in such a place will always be vulnerable to the possibility of someone stronger overwhelming them, and it is impossible to guarantee control over property in a world subject only to the rule of unlegitimated violence. In fact, nothing can be owned, and nothing can be considered wrong where there is no legitimate authority. In such a world, everybody would have as much right to everything as everyone else. Nothing could arbitrate between different wants. No ranking of competing needs could be explicable. Without instituted authority, there can be no injustice, and no right to exclusive property (Hobbes, 1996, p. 96).

This problem triggers the decision that inaugurates the second phase. In order to advance beyond this state into a world where natural human impulses can actually be fulfilled, human beings agree to cede government over themselves to some sovereign power. People realise that their self-interest lies most in abdicating their personal right-to-violence. Sovereign authority in some form—monarchic, oligarchic or perhaps even democratic—arrogates all social power to itself, pacifies society and guarantees personal and collective security. The state of nature that existed prior to the institution of sovereign power is a state of war "of every man, against every man" (Hobbes, 1996, p. 84). The commonwealth instituted to take its place as the alternative to war is peace.

Hobbes admits that this apparently diachronic narrative account is not to be taken literally, and that the state of nature and of commonwealth can be contemporary with one another. War, in fact, is to be understood not as actual fighting, but as the *possibility* of fighting. Hobbes writes, "so the nature of war, consisteth not in actual fighting, but in the known disposition thereto" (1996, p. 84). Peace is merely the "other time" when this is not the case, and is defined negatively, not as something with positive qualities itself, but as the absence of war. "All other time is PEACE," Hobbes writes (1996, p. 84). This complex relationship between war and peace requires some investigation. The point is that this disposition is not abolished or erased by the establishment of the commonwealth. It lingers. War for Hobbes does not represent a state of nature left behind in the patient human progress towards the civility of commonwealth. It is something back into which we could so easily slip "where there were no common power to fear" (Hobbes, 1996, p. 85). War *haunts* the commonwealth, permanently accompanying it, as the "disposition" that may undermine social cohesion, and against which sovereignty must be constantly vigilant. Richard E. Flathman outlines the various ways in which the state of nature and the commonwealth always co-exist (Flathman, 2002, p. 58). Overseeing all these convergences is the very logic by which the state of nature and the commonwealth, war and peace, always require one another for their identity and rationale. This may seem unsurprising, but has significant consequences for our practice of war and our dreams of peace.

It is usually thought that Hobbes sees humanity simply as egoistic. For example, he attributes the definition of morality purely to a logic of self-interest:

> But whatsoever is the object of any man's appetite or desire; that is it, which he for his part calleth *good*: and the object of his hate and aversion *evil*; and of his contempt, *vile* and *inconsiderable*. For these words of good, evil and contemptible, are ever used with relation to the person that useth them: there being nothing simply and absolutely so; nor any common rule of good and evil, to be taken from the nature of the objects themselves.
>
> (Hobbes, 1996, p. 35)

This argument assumes that moral judgement follows on from already established preferences: I want something in the world, and anything that satisfies this want or aids in my fulfilling it is good. The reverse is bad. The logic here seems quite clear: an existing subject identifies its wants and those things that aid to the satisfaction of those wants are approved, and those that do not come to be reviled.

Yet, Hobbes's argument actually exceeds this simple view. Desire is not simply an adjunct to life. It is indissociable from it:

> Continual success on obtaining those things which a man from time to time desireth, that is to say, continual prospering, is that men call FELICITY; I mean the felicity of this life. For there is no such thing as perpetual tranquillity of mind, while we live here; because life itself is but motion, and can never be without desire, nor without fear, no more than without sense.
>
> (Hobbes, 1996, p. 41)

A distinction then emerges between that which someone might desire "from time to time" and another kind of desire, a continual enduring one, one that life cannot be without. Desire here is both intermittent and something that endures co-extensively with uninterrupted life itself. In short, there is a distinction between desire as the repeated, but passing pursuit of one particular object after another, and desire as identical with life.

What is this second desire, this desire that endures beneath and beyond the drive to specific objects? First, it is that which makes the satisfaction acquired when you attain particular objects into something enduring. It is the desire that wants the happiness derived from attaining goals to continue indefinitely. In other words, it wants to transform the intermittent into the permanent. Yet, this perpetuation of pleasure rises above the objects one seeks, to become a desire for desire itself. In Hobbes's words: "the object of man's desire, is not to enjoy once only, and for one instant of time; but to assure forever, the way of his future desire" (1996, p. 66). Beneath the particular desires we have, and that are sometimes satisfied, we desire the perpetuation of desire itself.

Secondly, this desire for desire is thus the desire for the freedom of operation of desire, and thus the desire that I have the power to keep satisfying desires. It is a desire for power in the broadest sense of the word: "I put for a general inclination of all mankind, a perpetual and restless desire of power after power, that ceaseth only in death" (Hobbes, 1996, p. 66). This power, coextensive with life is not or not yet political power, but simply the desire for capacity, for the greatest possible freedom to fulfil one's desires:

> And the cause of this is not always that a man hopes for a more intensive delight, than he has already attained to; or that he cannot

be content with a moderate power: but because he cannot assure the power and means to live well, which he hath present, without the acquisition of more.

(Hobbes, 1996, p. 66)

What sets person against person, then, in the raw competition in the state of nature that is war, is the desire for ever greater capacity to fulfil unspecified desires: it is the desire for the power to gain greater power to fulfil desire. This is not the simple mechanism whereby an ego identifies the best way to pursue its already existing goals. It is not that we simply have goals and follow the urge to fulfil them. First and foremost, living itself is the endless extending of the possibility of having enough power to fulfil desire, whatever that desire might be. Life then is governed not by desire, but by the endless maximising of the possibility of ever more desire. Desire, then, and the power required to facilitate it are always larger than life, exceeding it, haunting it with the possibility of its necessary exaggeration. Desire is not about the pursuit of specific egoistic goals, but about the endless expansion of the capacity to desire more and more, to have more and more desire, whatever those desires may be. The state of war then is desire's desire for itself, manifested as individual people. War, according to Hobbes, then is hypothetical. It presses on us more in terms of how we anticipate it, rather than our literal practice of it. What is important is not the desires we have clearly identified and plan or manage to fulfil, it is our need to feel that our capacity to fulfil our desires is uncompromised, indeed expanding. The important thing is not what our desires are and how we can satisfy them, but that we have the sense that when desires will arise in the future we anticipate, we will by then be able to fulfil them, and that therefore we are now expanding our power to desire. In the state of nature, what matters is not the wars we have fought, but our anticipation of war, or our anticipation of readiness to fight the wars that might arise. Hobbes writes,

> there is no way for any man to secure himself, so reasonable, as anticipation; that is, by force, or wiles, to master the persons of all men he can, so long, till he see no other power great enough to endanger him: and this is no more than his own conservation requireth, and is generally allowed.
>
> (1996, p. 83)

At issue then is not the wars of the putative, imagined past from which we have ascended into the security of commonwealth, but the future that haunts our present, and that we must labour to control, or withstand:

> Also because there be some, that taking pleasure in contemplating their own power in the acts of conquest, which they pursue farther than their security requires; if others, that would be glad to be at ease within modest bounds, should not by invasion increase their own power, they would not be able, long time, by standing only on their defense, to subsist. And by consequence, such augmentation of dominion over men, being necessary to a man's conservation, it ought to be allowed him.
>
> (Hobbes, 1996, p. 83)

Survival, then, is not a business of merely defending oneself, or arranging, however ruthlessly, to get what you want. It means expanding one's power with only the possibility of war in mind, and with no knowable measure of how much power might ever be sufficient.

Both of the motives for struggle between individuals—competition caused by individuals in their need to satisfy their desires, and the need to defend oneself—rely on the construction of something hypothetical, indeed futuristic and imaginary. The third motive Hobbes identifies for violence is no more substantial: the need we have to be esteemed as highly by others as ourselves. Because he feels underestimated by his fellows, every man "naturally endeavours, as far as he dares...to extort a greater value from his contemners, by damage; and from others, by his example" (Hobbes, 1996, p. 83). We are at war then because of our open-ended need to secure our future: to have the capacity to fulfil our future desires; to have the power to withstand the possible attacks of others and to control the image we imagine to be held of us in the minds of others.

It is this series of mind-games and imaginings that create the state of nature. In other words, the state of nature is far from the brutal and truncated physical contest between bodies in an animalistic primitive violence. The struggle between human beings in the state of nature is a struggle over representations of possible futures. It is not about controlling a chaotic and unthinking violence which we always automatically find ourselves practising. It is in fact about the way we imagine violence might occur and plan to organise ourselves to either control or benefit from it:

> For WAR, consisteth not in battle only, or the act of fighting; but in a tract of time, wherein the will to contend by battle is sufficiently

known: and therefore the notion of *time*, is to be considered in the nature of war; as it is in the nature of weather. For as the nature of foul weather, lieth not in a shower or two of rain; but in an inclination thereto of many days together: so the nature of war, consisteth not in actual fighting; but in the known disposition thereto, during all the time there is no assurance to the contrary.

(Hobbes, 1996, p. 84)

Here, what is important is the future as the opening of possibility: what is at stake is not the experience of the flood, but the fact that rain may fall on a cloudy day. In the state of nature, we live not in a state of inundation, but anticipation. It is not the ever-present reality of violence pressing in on us that makes us call out for security, but the fact that we can imagine a future violence. It is not the brutality of our physical reality that makes life "solitary, poor, nasty, brutish and short" (p. 84) but our ability to conceive of time.

The diachronic reading of Hobbes which sees the state of nature as the condition from which we have advanced into the higher state of assured and secure civil society is a misreading therefore. The conception of time in Hobbes is one of anticipation, not retrospection. That is why the examples he repeatedly gives of the state of nature are contemporary, not historical: how "the savage people in many places of America...live at this day" (p. 85); how "men that have formerly lived under a peaceful government...degenerate...in a civil war" (p. 85) or indeed how "in all times, kings, and persons of sovereign authority...are in continual jealousies, and in the state and posture of gladiators...which is a posture of war" (p. 85).

The state of nature, then, is not something to be overcome. It defines our sense of the future, and thus remains with us. It *is* our sense of the future, not a primitive residue of our primeval past. This is confirmed by the fact that the commonwealth is not actually instituted to overcome the state of nature but to fulfil its primary law. If the war of all against all springs from the desire to secure one's desire, then it becomes obvious that this goal is unattainable in the state of nature: "as long as this natural right of every man to every thing endureth, there can be no security to any man (how strong or wise soever he be)" (Hobbes, 1996, p. 87). As a result, it soon becomes apparent that life is best secured by peace, and war only makes sense if peace fails. Not only is peace clearly preferable to war as a way of securing what one wants, but abdication of one's prerogative emerges as a clear path to securing one's desire. If the first law of nature is to secure oneself through peace rather than war, the second is this "that a man be willing, when others are so too, as far-forth, as for peace, and defense of himself as he shall think it necessary, to lay down this right to all things" (p. 87). Since the absolute state of nature can never guarantee ownership nor justice, the only way to facilitate one's desire is to modify it by way of concessions to other people. These concessions will inevitably become enlarged into the institution of the commonwealth, based on a paradoxical logic: no power without abdicating power, no fulfilment of desire without some ceding of desire. This allows for the complex and nuanced view of nature in Hobbes: it is both that which impels us to contrive sovereign power and that which sovereign power must supersede; that which sovereign power controls, but also, what it deploys in relation to other sovereign powers. Self-interest calls out for sovereignty to both control and fulfil it, inhibit and allow it in the one act. The drive to self-preservation is what defined us in the state of nature, but it is also what motivates us to formalise and legalise a power over us: "The final cause, end, or design of men…in the introduction of that restraint upon themselves (in which we see them live in commonwealths,) is the foresight of their own preservation" (Hobbes, 1996, p. 111).

In short, then, the institution of the commonwealth aims to achieve what was sought in the state of nature—the perpetuation of the life of desire (life-as-desire)—in time, understood as the anticipation and planning for possibility. Possibility, here, is defined in double terms as both, on the one hand, the endless enlargement of desire and as the risk of our life being overtaken by the disposition to war, on the other. The state of nature responds to and encourages desire but cannot fulfil it, because the disposition to war always threatens. The commonwealth by proposing to control the disposition to war can guarantee that desire can be at least hypothetically fulfilled. Desire is meaningless in the state of nature which would seem its appropriate place, because the threat of chaos and violence makes securing the object and perpetuation of desire impossible. There can be no secure property in the state of nature. War then makes the fulfilment of the desire that explains it impossible. War is implicitly in contradiction with itself.

We cannot call the commonwealth peace. As we have seen peace has no positive definition in Hobbes. It is merely that which is other to war, and this otherness is not really one of opposition. Indeed, the commonwealth is instituted in order to make the dream of war—the fulfilment of desire—possible. The commonwealth thus is also in contradiction with itself. It is not only instituted by war, but in the service of the very goals that war was supposed to, but cannot, fulfil. The commonwealth is the successful version of war. In sum, the relationship between the commonwealth and the state of nature is not one of opposition. Instead, the relationship causes both the commonwealth and the state of nature to be in contradiction with themselves. As we have seen, war in the state of nature unfolds as a way not of fulfilling specific desires but of maximising the possibility of desire's expanding beyond itself, the impulse that was life. In the commonwealth, then, war is seen as the excess of the possibility of a limitless desire over desire. It is the gap between desire as realisable and the possibility that desire generates as the principle of life. In the commonwealth, we give up life for what we desire. We find a way to make the potential infinity of desire livable, but we endlessly pay tribute to the beckoning horizon of an infinite desire, knowing that no specific desire would be possible without it. Every act of peace still gestures towards war.

The commonwealth is not imposed on humanity, but is an act and expression of it. Yet it cannot be a collective act of humanity, because it arises before there can be a collective. It is the act of separate individuals that allows them to form a collective for the first time, one in which their individual wills are both fulfilled and denied. Hobbes puts it like this:

> The only way to erect such a common power, as may be able to defend them from the invasion of foreigners, and the injuries of one another, and thereby to secure them in such sort, as that by their own industry, and by the fruits of the earth, they may nourish themselves and live contentedly; is, to confer all their power and strength upon one man, or, upon one assembly of men, that may reduce all their wills, by plurality of voices, unto one will: which is as much as to say, to appoint one man, or assembly of men, to bear their person.
> (1996, p. 114)

The fulfilment of our desire only becomes possible in the peaceful space made available by the institution of the commonwealth which simultaneously reduces our multiplicity to a singularity. Our individuality is fulfilled by its denial in the submission of our will to a singular authority. Yet this submission is not the retreat of the individual into passivity. It is the possibility of the individual's own action, because every individual must "own, and acknowledge himself to be author of whatsoever he that so beareth their person, shall act, or cause to be acted, in those things which concern the common peace and safety; and therein to submit their wills, every one to his will, and their judgements, to his judgement" (Hobbes, 1996, p. 114). The individual is not only given the possibility of fulfilling desire by resigning it, but acts only by giving up power: individuals have submitted to power by making themselves "every one the author" (p. 114) of it: "by this institution of a commonwealth, every particular man is author of all the sovereign doth" (p. 117).

Sovereign power then is instituted in order to control excess, the excess of desire over desire that is life. Yet, sovereign power is itself "unlimited," indivisible (Hobbes, 1996, p. 216) and exceptional. Even though so "unlimited a power" (p. 138) may terrify us with the possibility of evil or tyrannical consequences, it is better than the "perpetual war of every man against his neighbour," which is "much worse" (p. 138). Sovereign power is itself therefore always in excess of the individual wills that institute it. It is both that which limits the self-fulfilment of individuals and that which allows it. It is both the apotheosis of their liberty and its contradiction. In a discussion of the relationship between liberty and necessity, Hobbes argues that paradoxically the liberty of individuals is only possible as an expression of the sovereign necessity of God's will: "And therefore, God, that seeth, and disposeth all things, seeth also that the *liberty* of man in doing what he will, is accompanied by the *necessity* of doing that which God will, and no more, nor less" (p. 140).

Human liberty fulfils divine necessity therefore. The relationship to the sovereign is analogous: "The liberty of a subject, lieth therefore only in those things, which in regulating their actions, the sovereign hath praetermitted" (p. 141). The liberty of the individual therefore is realised in relationship to the unlimited and excessive power of the sovereign, even to the point of death. In fact, the power of life and death of the sovereign over the individual is to be seen as the fulfilment of the individual's liberty:

> we are not to understand, that by [individual] liberty, the sovereign power of life, and death, is either abolished, or limited. For it has been already shown, that nothing the sovereign representative can do to a subject, on what pretence soever, can properly be called injustice or injury; because every subject is author of every act the sovereign doth; so that he never wanteth right to any thing, otherwise, than as he himself is the subject of God, and bound thereby to observe the laws of nature. And therefore it may, and doth often happen in commonwealths, that a subject may be put to death, by the command of the sovereign power.
> (Hobbes, 1996, pp. 141–2)

In the state of nature the individual had not sought simply to fulfil its desire, but to maximise its hypothetical and future ability to keep doing so. Desire becomes coextensive with life as the ability to empower the facilitation of individual desire. This was the putative end of individual action: the excess of life over desire.

In the commonwealth, this contradiction between life and desire results in the sacrifice of the excessive and endless possibility of the fulfilment of desire—now recognised as identical with the disposition to war, and thus the limitation of the practical ability to fulfil desire—in the name of the specific desires that only the commonwealth can guarantee to be met. Yet, the commonwealth only does this as itself the excess over the fulfilment of specific desires. And, as "life" had been in the state of nature, this excess is the always excessive, irreducible fulfilment of the individual's action, whose aim in instituting sovereign power was always simply to make the fulfilment of desire possible. In other words, in the state of nature, life promised the fulfilment of desire while being the always irreducible excess over desire. The situation in the commonwealth is the same, except now the sovereign has taken the place of life. Sovereignty, then, has taken war's place as the endlessly renewed promise of the fulfilment of desire as the enactment of the individual's will.

Sovereignty then is the double of war, its twin, pair and analogy. It delivers what war promises, but cannot achieve. It instantiates the individual will that the state of nature encouraged and licensed but could not realise. It does not elude war, and produce a higher state of development that leaves war behind. It succeeds where war fails. It does what war claims as its own, but cannot actually achieve. It is war despite itself. The war it defies and abominates, ridicules and defeats, always remains its meaning.

It is clear that for Hobbes, war and its other, civil society under the authority of the sovereign, must be defined in relation to one another. At one level, this is a relationship of contradiction: we institute civil order so as to escape war, our natural state. Yet the function of civil society is to make possible the fulfilment of desire that defines nature, and that nature itself cannot fulfil. Civil society, and indeed sovereign authority itself, therefore, do war's work, while attempting to quell it. We live in societies defined by their antipathy to war, but that always think of war as their perpetual companion, something perpetually tempting us with the possibility of enacting what it is that we really want. We refuse war, but animate it constantly, constantly turning towards it, thinking of it, requiring it, despite ourselves.

Kant: Peace through war

Kant's argument in *Perpetual Peace* seems at first to share much with Hobbes. They both see peace and political authority as instituted to withstand a naturally existing state of war which is more primitive. Both see the fixed principles of human nature as constituting the relationship between war and civil society. Yet significant differences emerge between them, first about the fundamental nature of what these principles actually are, but also about the nature of how the relationship between war and peace extends into society. We have seen how for Hobbes, the sovereign fulfils what was hoped for in war, by supplanting it. The sovereign remains the inverted double of war. We will see another doubleness in Kant, one that persists in entangling war in peace, but instead of peace fulfilling what war seeks, now peace will be seen as only possible through war. Yet at the same time, war must be seen as that which defies peace by its very nature. War then opposes and resists peace, but is the only thing that can make peace possible.

We saw how in Hobbes, nature triggered in human beings the determination to pursue self-interest. At first, it seems that the clearest way to pursue this self-interest is in an immediate and ruthless competition, the war of all against all. Soon, however, it becomes apparent that these goals can only really be met by social combination and submission to a sovereign authority: sacrifice of self leads to the possible fulfilment of self. Sovereignty can make possible what was sought but ultimately unattainable in pre-social isolation. In Kant, the situation is quite different. It is true that war seems "natural" to humanity—"War itself requires no special motive but appears to be grafted on human nature; it passes even for something noble, to which the love of glory impels men quite apart from any selfish urges" (Kant, 1957, pp. 28–9). Both of these motives had been recognised by Hobbes (1996, p. 83). However, Kant disputes the purely egotistical understanding of humanity in Hobbes. This emerges in their different accounts of the origin of the moral. Where Hobbes had seen morality purely as a declension of self-interest ("For these words of good, evil, and contemptible, are ever used with relation to the person that useth them": Hobbes, 1996, p. 35), Kant sees morality as emerging through reason, and perfecting its universal and impersonal work: "Taken objectively, morality is in itself practical, being the totality of unconditionally mandatory laws according to which we ought to act" (Kant, 1957, p. 35). As the logic by which we must live, morality must be able to be fulfilled:

> It would obviously be absurd, after granting authority to the concept of duty, to pretend that we cannot do our duty, for in that case this concept would itself drop out of morality...Consequently, there can be no conflict of politics, as a practical doctrine of right, with ethics, as a theoretical doctrine of right.
>
> (Kant, 1957, p. 35)

In this sense, it is separate from self-interest:

> there is no conflict of practice with theory, unless by ethics we mean a general doctrine of prudence, which can be the same as a theory of the maxims for choosing the most fitting means to accomplish the purposes of self-interest. But to give this meaning to ethics is equivalent to denying that there is any such thing at all.
>
> (p. 35)

To Kant, therefore, human beings do not construct morality in order to rationalise and justify their desires. In its impersonality and universalism, morality requires that political authority be regulated according to the precepts of practical reason. Sovereign authority may have been instituted only by the stronger: "we can count on nothing but force to establish the juridical condition, on the compulsion of which public law will later be established" (Kant, 1957, p. 36). But the "possibility" of a unity between morality and politics "must be conceded" (p. 37). Indeed, although the intention to form society may spring from pragmatism, in the end, social organisation must become subject to the rigours of duty. The prudence which established society as the best means for human beings to attain their goals must give way to the order of practical reason. What Kant here phrases in terms of individual states holds for all individuals:

> political maxims must not be derived from the welfare or happiness which a single state expects from obedience to them, and thus not from the end which one of them proposes for itself. That is, they must not be deduced from volition as the supreme yet empirical principle of political wisdom, but rather from the pure concept of the duty of right, from the *ought* whose principle is given a priori by pure reason, regardless of what the physical consequences may be.
>
> (Kant, 1957, p. 45)

This puts Kant in opposition to Hobbes. Where for Hobbes, the goal both of the war of all against all and of the eventual construction of the commonwealth was the fulfilment of human desire, indeed the opening to the possibility of desire extending over time—desire for desire—in Kant, society is formed because of the actions of force imposing order on human chaos, but this force must eventually subordinate itself to the universal logic of morality. Morality must be fulfilled regardless of whether this has beneficial results: "All politics must bend its knee before the right" (Kant, 1957, p. 46).

Kant then establishes an opposition between, on the one hand, prudence, which seeks practical goals, and, on the other hand, duty, which demands conformity to moral logic. Indeed, he goes so far as to claim that though it may seem odd, the only way to achieve the goals prudence seeks is by way of subordination to duty:

> For it is the peculiarity of morals, especially with respect to the principles of public law and hence in relation to politics known a priori, that the less it makes conduct depend on the proposed end, i.e., the intended material or moral advantage, the more it agrees with it in general. This is because it is the universal will given a priori... which determines the relations among men, and if practice consistently follows it, this will can also, by the mechanism of nature, cause the desired result and make the concept of law effective. So, for instance, it is a principle of moral politics that a people should unite into a state according to juridical concepts of freedom and equality, and this principle is based not on prudence but on duty.
>
> (Kant, 1957, pp. 43–4)

If the desired result is itself moral and thus in conformity with universal will, then submission to the authority of universal will bring it about, without it necessarily being directly aimed at. Peace, for example, will not be achieved directly, as a distinctive and isolated goal of our plans and schemes. It will emerge inevitably and indirectly by way of our commitment to universal moral reason: "Then it may be said: 'Seek ye first the kingdom of pure practical reason and its righteousness, and your end (the blessing of perpetual peace) will necessarily follow'" (Kant, 1957, p. 43).

It is not, therefore, that Kant simply puts duty in contradiction with peace as a human priority. It is not that duty must be followed, and if either war or peace is the consequence, then so be it. Peace remains Kant's priority, and not any peace, *perpetual peace*. What emerges is that peace is so identified with the logic of pure practical reason in its subsistence as duty that peace will inevitably follow from the commitment to duty. What this means is that peace is so identified with the moral law, that the very absence of the moral law is equivalent to a state of war. This idea emerges clearly in Kant's discussion of the contrast between peace and the mere cessation of hostilities (a theme revisited by Levinas, as we shall see). Kant writes,

> The state of peace among men living side by side is not the natural state (*status naturalis*); the natural state is one of war. A state of peace,

therefore, must be *established*, for in order to be secured against hostility it is not sufficient that hostilities simply be not committed; and, unless this security is pledged to each by his neighbour (a thing that can occur only in a civil state), each may treat his neighbour, from whom he commands this security as an enemy.

(1957, p. 10)

Here, we have another version of Hobbes's idea that it was not war itself, but the "known disposition" (Hobbes, 1996, p. 84) to it that counts. For Kant, the mere absence of hostilities is insufficient to guarantee peace. This is a theme he will pick up again in discussing treaties of peace, which, if they are mere pretexts by which the warring parties regroup and reconsider their advantage in order to make war again at a later date, are obviously not peace at all (Kant, 1957, p. 18). This entanglement of war and peace, or identification of pseudo-peaces, is important in Kant, and elsewhere. The distinction between war and peace is nothing if not problematic. In practical terms, the two may not be separable, even for Kant (as we shall soon see!)

Peace, then, truly relies, not just on a mere lull in fighting, but on some deeper "pledge." It is not actual violence that defines the state of war; nor is it even the possibility of violence that we have encountered in Hobbes. The very co-habitation of human beings in a state of lawlessness is sufficient to be the violence of war: "Man (or the people) in the state of nature deprives me, by this mere status of his, even though he does not injure me actively (*facto*); he does so by the lawlessness of his condition (*statu iniusto*) which constantly threatens me" (Kant, 1957, p. 10). It is thus law itself that guarantees peace. War is not violence, real or potential. It is lawlessness, whatever form it takes. "All men who can reciprocally influence each other must stand under some civil constitution" (p. 10). The language here is telling. War is the possibility of reciprocal influence without law. Violence itself does not necessarily count, as even the absence of violence may merely be a regrouping to consolidate strategic advantage, as we have seen. Kant demotes the importance of violence in the definition of war, since the latter may continue even through the very forms of peace and co-habitation. In short, then, Kant replaces the contrast between war and peace, between violence and quiet, or between nature and commonwealth, with the contrast between lawlessness and law, into which all the previous dichotomies are to be subsumed.

The problem here is potentially immense, and may lead to historical consequences Kant did not imagine. If obeisance to duty and reason becomes more important than the suppression of violence in the definition and delivery of peace, then duty replaces the suppression of violence as the meaning of peace. The problem of war becomes not the problem of carnage and atrocity, of physical brutality, of literal *killing*, but the violation of moral order. It is not so far, then, from this point to the reversal of the relationship between war and peace: peace becomes separable from non-violence, since the latter is not necessarily in conformity to the law (given that we can still be in a state of war if we are outside the law, even if we are not fighting). On the other hand, if the law becomes not only the implicit guarantee of peace, but its *meaning*, then violence which may facilitate the operation of the law may be a means to attain peace. Kant writes of the person with whom I co-habit the state of lawlessness: "I can compel him either to enter with me into a state of civil law or to remove himself from my neighbourhood" (Kant, 1957, p. 10). In other words, I can use force in order to implement the civil law that is the meaning of peace. From our pre-emptive invasions to moralistic Second World War nostalgia movies, from pious slogans about freedom to the rhetoric of triumph and historical vindication we live out in our computer-games, this implicit identification between morality and peace licenses fighting for the good, wars for peace, a perpetual peace indistinguishable perhaps from the hell with which warriors threaten their benighted and degraded enemies.

We have seen above that Kant understood the formation of the civil society that would come to allow for the institution of moral law, as something delivered by force:

> since a uniting force must supervene upon the variety of particular volitions in order to produce a common will from them, establishing this whole is something no one individual in the group can perform; hence in the practical execution of this idea we can count on nothing but force to establish the juridical condition, on the compulsion of which public law will later be established.
>
> (Kant, 1957, p. 36)

Only force makes the establishment of the law possible. This is true internationally as much as it is in civil society:

> Peoples, as states, like individuals, may be judged to injure one another merely by their coexistence in the state of nature (i.e., while independent of external laws). Each of them may and should for

the sake of its own security demand that the others enter with it into a constitution similar to the civil constitution, for under such a constitution each can be secure in his right.

(Kant, 1957, p. 16)

In short, peace can be effected by force because peace is not itself inalienably equivalent to non-violence. Peace is itself the operation of established law. The establishment of the rule of law rests on the formation of civil society by force. The "juridical condition" can be established only by a force imposed on our several wills. Law then rides on force, or is instituted by force. Peace is instituted by violence to ward off a state of lawlessness that is constantly open to war, even equivalent to it, whether it is violent or not.

Kant develops this argument in an historical account of how peace always emerges only through war. This emerges in the "First Supplement" to *Perpetual Peace*, entitled "Of the Guarantee for Perpetual Peace." Kant argues, contrary to the idea that the state of nature is implicitly violent, that it is nature itself that guarantees perpetual peace: "her aim is to produce a harmony among men, against their will and indeed through their discord...working according to laws we do not know" (Kant, 1957, p. 24).

This apparently works in three stages: first, nature has made the whole of the earth inhabitable; secondly, nature has allowed people to be driven into the most remote corners of the earth by wars and thirdly, again by war, nature has made people enter into "more or less" lawful relations with one another. Peace, then, emerges only after war, after the scattering of peoples and their realisation that only lawfulness will allow them to survive together. War must be tried first in order for these lessons to be learnt. This is how Kant deals with the claim he repeats elsewhere that war is natural to human beings. Nature makes people fight wars because its goal is peace. War is the only means by which people can learn that peace is better. Therefore, war is nature's own means for advancing peace. War, if you like, defeats itself to establish peace. But we must go through war first, in the same way the only means by which the law can be established—the law that will institute peace—is by force. Force and violence, even in their most generalised form as war, are the means to peace. The meaning of war is peace.

Nature then delivers peace despite what people might think and want. The law is our duty, but peace is not. Peace arises through an impersonal operation of nature, over and above what moral choices we might make:

> If I say of nature that she wills that this or that might occur, I do not mean that she imposes a duty on us to do it, for this can be done by free practical reason; rather I mean that she herself does it whether we will it or not.
>
> (Kant, 1957, p. 29)

Peace is our destiny (p. 24), not our choice. It is not something we decide on or enact for ourselves. In fact, it seems that if we ourselves seek peace, we would then frustrate the unfolding of the war through which peace will actually be delivered. In other words, we must fight wars, or give into our natural impulse for war, because this is the way peace will become available, almost incidentally. Indeed, the first way in which we are converted to peace is by way of the combinations we must organise in order to be effective fighters:

> Even if a people were not forced by internal discord to submit to public laws, war would compel them to do so, for we have already seen that nature has placed each people near another which presses upon it, and against this it must form itself into a state of order to defend itself.
>
> (Kant, 1957, p. 29)

War then will be defeated in the process by which we organise to fight. In other words, war will already be defeated even as we go out to fight. It will be advanced and surpassed in the one act. By balancing out the conflicting self-interests in a given society, the imposition of the general law that makes a people ready to fight war opens up the possibility of peace:

> it does not require that we know how to attain the moral improvement of men but only that we should know the mechanism of nature in order to use it on men, organising the conflict of the hostile intentions present in a people in such a way that they must compel themselves to submit to coercive laws. Thus a state of peace is established in which laws have force.
>
> (Kant, 1957, p. 30)

It is not only then that law is established by force, but that peace is established by actual preparation for fighting. Without war there would be no peace, therefore. Perpetual peace will be attained when the lessons of war have been learnt and its gift institutionalised. This would be when we have already fought wars, and learnt from them not only their destructiveness, but what they reveal about the necessity of co-operation.

Peace, then, is a consequence of war. The argument would seem to be that the thing that actually convinces us to overcome our individual differences in order to submit to the rule of law as a group is the fact that we are being attacked from the outside. Our solidarity in the formation of a legal social group therefore involves suppressing internal differences because we are being attacked. What this means is that the solidarity of the group is not a result of some shared identification with one another, but rather because we are being treated as a single entity by somebody else. Our solidarity as a group, our identity, therefore, emerges because we are perceived as a group by others. This weakens the implied claim that what has been achieved in the transition from individuals into nation states can be accomplished by analogous actions on the part of nation states to form a single world community. Outside of science fiction, this kind of event is pure imagination. Only the unfolding of reason then could make the organisation of a global community of law assurable. The historical evolution then that would make the solidarity of individual states together a mere analogy to the solidarity that made individuals into nation states does not seem guaranteed. The symmetry of Kant's historical narrative is not assured.

Nation states form then according to a discipline imposed on them because they are attacked from the outside. This then makes them realise the advantages of a life under law. The social bond here would seem weak, and only the triumph of reason allows difference to be overcome. What this means is that individual differences—the state of war—are not so much overcome as held in check by the state. This indeed is why Kant believes the Republican is the preferable form of constitution, because "the powers of each selfish inclination are so arranged in opposition that one moderates or destroys the ruinous effect of the other" (p. 30). The struggle between competing preferences endures into social organisation. Its effects may be moderated, but what existed as the state of nature or war can still be met under constituted society, simply in a form that can be controlled. This again challenges the idea of a "perpetual peace," one that we will one day enter into as a stage of human development that leaves war behind.

War is not violence, but simply people living together in a lawless state. Peace is the rule of law that is imposed by force. We are justified in using force in order to compel other people to submit to the rule of reason that will guarantee perpetual peace. This imposition by force of peace may also take the form of a war imposed on us from the outside, which convinces us to suppress social competition because solidarity has military advantages. It is the military advantages of solidarity that assure us that the state of nature or war is a bad thing. War for Kant is dissociated from violence. War is merely lawlessness, regardless of whether violence takes place or not. In fact, war overcomes war to guarantee perpetual peace.

War and peace in Kant are entangled in one another. The idea of a perpetual peace built only on war, and indeed a social peace that manages by reason but that does not eradicate the natural will to war, means that the historical narrative that sees peace as built on a war it leaves behind, first in the passage from individualism to sociality and from society to global commonweal, never settles into a purposeful sequence. War in Kant forms peace. Peace requires war. War is never left behind by peace, nor vice versa.

We have seen in Hobbes and Kant two versions of the idea that war and civil society contradict one another. Yet, as this argument is developed, a far more complex position develops, one in which war and its other are in a much more complex relationship. In Hobbes, sovereign authority and the order it administers supplant war but only by offering what war seemed to offer, but could not deliver. In Kant, peace also transcends war, but only through it. Do these arguments simply reveal, despite the avowed intentions of their authors and their subsequent reputations, that, in fact, there is no contrast between war and civil society? Are the two simply one dynamic in simple co-ordinated operation, in one neat, unbroken sequence from intention to execution? The most famous version of this view resides in Western culture's most famous and most cited theorist of war, Carl von Clausewitz, to whom we now turn.

Clausewitz: War as the activation of the social

No statement about war seems less ambiguous—or is more often quoted—than Carl von Clausewitz's "War is a mere continuation of policy by other means" (Clausewitz, 1968, p. 119). Since its appearance in Clausewitz's posthumously published *On War* (1832), this has become the most canonical conception of war in the western tradition, bringing it out from the shadows of art, ritual and authority into the logic of politics and planning. War, according to this formulation, seems to be a denomination of intention, but not the intention of generals and warriors. War, here, is not a space in which politics and diplomacy break down, leaving the field open to trial by brute force and the cunning of the enigmatic warriors who inhabit the margins of social life. War, in Clausewitz's formulation, is not the place in which politics reaches its limit and hands over the future to some other means of determination. War is simply one tool of policy, a means of securing advantage when more respectable, civil means fail to secure for you what you want. It is this cool, perhaps cynical, formulation of war that has provided the touchstone for the modern inclusion of war in the logic of social life, from *Realpolitik* to Foucault's cute reversal of Clausewitz, which we will look at in some detail later.

If war is not the point where the logic of political rationality breaks down in chaos and violence, if it is not the place where the merely primitive interrupts the meaningful calculation of peaceful benefit and order, if it is not the place where sovereignty loses its grip and gives way to the war of each against all, if it is in fact, the activation of political intention, then it ceases to be the opposite of social life, or that which social life labours to exclude, and becomes the execution of definitively social values. In other words, it becomes the expression of a certain political order, and is thus exemplary of the unfolding of political order in general. It is a social activity. It is not an arcane or remote practice. It is not esoteric. Clausewitz writes,

> We say therefore War belongs not to the province of Arts and Sciences, but to the province of social life. It is a conflict of great interests which is settled by bloodshed, and only in that is it different from others. It would be better, instead of comparing it with any Art, to liken it to business competition, which is also a conflict of human interests and activities; and it is still more like a State policy, which again on its part, may be looked upon as a kind of business competition on a great scale. Besides, State policy is the womb in which War is developed, in which its outlines lie hidden in a rudimentary state, like the qualities of living creatures in their germs.
> (Clausewitz, 1968, pp. 202–3)

War is only distinguished from other social conflicts because it is on a greater scale, and because it ends in bloodshed. Social life is to be understood as a site of conflict even in its most elementary and recognisable form, the daily operation of commerce, itself a "conflict of human interests and activities." War then is not mysterious and foreign. It does not arise from another moral or psychological domain. It is not madness interrupting order; nor is it a point in which arcane rituals supersede daily life. It is part of daily life, violent yes, and on a great scale, but banal, worldly and knowable, transparent and immediately recognisable as a mere version of what we are doing here now all the time anyway. It is the offspring, the forthcoming of society.

Yet, as we shall see, this is not the only conception of war in Clausewitz. There is another war, a war of passion, "ideal war" (Clausewitz, 1968,

p. 120), the war that somehow tends towards itself, towards the maximum expression of energy, towards full hostility and the will towards the annihilation of the enemy. The energy that this other war releases is a social energy too. It is, above all, fuelled by the passion of the people, whose motivation threatens the cool calculation of policy, or the unknowable and admirable intuitive genius of the great general, by inserting into war a force difficult to rationalise. The wars of the Napoleonic and post-Napoleonic era are defined for Clausewitz by the way they bring these two wars together: the refinement of rational policy in the hands of the military genius, on the one hand, and the massive potentially revolutionary energy of the people, on the other. It is here that the canonical promoter of the logic of social purpose in war prefigures, perhaps augurs, the total wars to come a century later.

This account of war in Clausewitz amplifies the argument that war is an *activation* of the social. War is not symptomatic or representative of some particular aspect of social meaning here. It is not an indication of the nature of society or of humanity in general. It is not part of a model of human nature, a model that includes war with sociality as its necessary complement or competitor. War is an animation of society, in part and then as a whole, as policy and then as passion, as strategy, then as energy, ultimately as both working together to make modern war possible. War, for Clausewitz, is not to be seen as an indication of something about humanity's metaphysical nature, nor about the definition of the structure of the social. It is not an abstraction nor an idea. It is not a clue to something else. It is a style of practices in which society unleashes its energy and enacts its interest. It is a behaviour, not an essence, a tool not a state, a means not a meaning.

I want now to study the complexities of Clausewitz's account of war, by looking first at the logic of war as policy, and the enigmatic military genius in whom it is best entrusted. Then I will look at the idea that seems to contradict this account of war: the idea of war as an intense, energetic will to hostility, what Clausewitz calls war in its abstract or ideal form, and then finally how these different wars have come together in Clausewitz's own era. In this combination of intensity and rationality, what becomes possible is a conception of the intimacy of war and social life, of war as society in action.

According to Clausewitz, rational war must control the violence of the population who must fight, but more importantly it must also clarify our thinking about war. We must understand that war is not the suspension of policy, but its most meaningful implementation:

> We know, certainly, that war is only called forth through the political intercourse of Governments and Nations; but in general it is supposed that such intercourse is broken off by War, and that a totally different state of things ensues, subject to no laws but its own.
>
> (Clausewitz, 1968, p. 402)

It is a mistake to consider war the failure or lapse of diplomacy. War is in fact a specific version of diplomacy:

> War is nothing but a continuation of political intercourse, with a mixture of other means. We say mixed with other means in order thereby to maintain at the same time that this political intercourse does not cease by the War itself, is not changed into something quite different, but that, in its essence, it continues to exist, whatever may be the form of the means which it uses, and that the chief lines on which the events of the war progress, and to which they are attached, are only the general features of policy which run all through the War until peace takes place. And how can we conceive it to be otherwise? Does the cessation of diplomatic notes stop the political relations between different Nations and Governments? Is not War merely another kind of writing and language for political thoughts? It has certainly a grammar of its own, but its logic is not peculiar to itself.
>
> (Clausewitz, 1968, p. 402)

Diplomacy does not give way to war or even simply slip into it. Diplomacy switches to war as another grammar in which its meaning can be expressed. War is a diplomatic note materialised as "other means." This war imposes a rational logic from above. War is a top-down organisation of society's vital impulses and their subordination to calculation and purpose. Diplomacy is a delicate game in one context, of notes, unformulated understandings and cynical even deceitful temporary alliances. That war should be one of diplomacy's modes seems unsurprising. What is crucial is the way diplomacy and purpose can bring violence within their orbit. Not only can they, but they must. This top-down war in Clausewitz's hands is not just the best way to understand how war takes place, but it is the model of war he recommends. It is not simply what war is, but what it should be, if we are sensible:

> No War is commenced, or, at least, no War should be commenced, if people acted wisely, without first seeking a reply to this question, What is to be attained by and in the same? The first is the final object; the other is the intermediate aim. By this chief consideration the whole course of the war is prescribed, the extent of the means and the measure of energy are determined; its influence manifests itself down to the smallest organ of action.
> (Clausewitz, 1968, p. 367)

This war is rational and elite, descending not only from the above of governments but the more natural or cosmic Romantic above of genius.

In Clausewitz, there is a match between the intense and elaborate calculation of rational factors and purpose on the one hand, and inexplicable individual genius on the other. It is here where we gain insight into how the diplomatic war is actually mounted. War requires calculation and prediction. A vast number of factors have to be taken into consideration in working out the advantages and disadvantages of a particular campaign. These calculations are not simple arithmetic but require the kind of invisible, mysterious and super-human ability that everywhere at this time was being seen as the apogee of human cultural achievement, the point where the mystery of subjectivity intrudes most tellingly into human affairs while keeping its logic cloaked: genius:

> In order to ascertain the real scale of the means which we must put forth for War, we must think over the political object both on our own side and on the enemy's side; we must consider the power and position of the enemy's State as well as of our own, the character of his Government and of his people, and the capacities of both, and all that again on our own side, and the political connection of other States, and the effect which the War will produce on those States. That the determination of these diverse circumstances and their diverse connexions with each other is an immense problem, that it is the true flash of genius which discovers here in a moment what is right, and that it would be quite out of the question to become master of the complexity merely by a methodical study, it is easy to conceive.
> (Kant, 1957, p. 375)

War instigated by diplomatic need requires rich observation and calculation. Yet there is nothing simply arithmetic about these calculations. Obscure variables of profit and loss, of more and less involve not only guesswork, but speculative evaluation. Who is capable of such insight? This is not something that can be taught. It requires reason but cannot be accomplished simply by a method that can be shared. Rational war may be. Simply calculable it is not.

The genius carries within him the totality of the world he must evaluate. He must not only enact war through the fury of intense but unknowable calculations, but must himself be an incarnation of the unfolding logic of war:

> The moral reaction, the ever-changeful form of things, makes it necessary for the chief actor to carry in himself the whole mental apparatus of his knowledge, that anywhere and at every pulse-beat he may be capable of giving the requisite decision from himself.
> (Clausewitz, 1968, p. 200)

The genius is himself full of war and determines what should happen at each particular moment, not only by himself, but *from* himself. Strategy is a pouring forth of the nature of his genius, because his genius is produced out of a reservoir of knowledge and experience animated as a complete mental apparatus vivified as the pulse-beat of his very life. War becomes him, becomes itself genius in him.

Genius may be mysterious but it is part of the logic of civilisation. The uncivilised tribes may have a disposition to warfare. This is obvious, but genius is not available to them:

> Amongst uncivilised people, we never find a truly great General, and very seldom what we can properly call a military genius, because that requires a development of the intelligent powers which cannot be found in an uncivilised State.... The greatest names... that have been renowned in War belong strictly to epochs of higher culture.
> (Clausewitz, 1968, p. 139)

War in Clausewitz, here, is more than an account of cool and cynical decisions. It is a theory of civilisation. It is too easy to reduce his work to the simple assertion of the importance of determining advantage in the big-picture game of diplomacy, and a single gnomic statement. What is important in Clausewitz, however, is the thoroughness of his model of human society. It is all very well to say that war is simply an extension of diplomacy, but how does this come to enact itself in the world? The answer is through the being of the military genius, rational operation shapes chaos into purpose. Only genius is capable of this, and only the advanced epochs of culture and civilisation are capable of genius.

What are they working with? The other side of the coin is the animation and energy of the people themselves. Here, something curious emerges. War is defined in a second way in *On War*, and it is in fact the primary definition. Genius emerges *after* something else, what Clausewitz calls "ideal" war and shapes it, subordinating it to policy. As we have seen, uncivilised peoples are capable of war, but they are not capable of genius. The first definition of war that Clausewitz offers is this: "War...is an act of violence intended to compel our opponent to fulfil our will" (Clausewitz, 1968, p. 101). He goes on, "Violence, that is to say, physical force...is...the *means*; the compulsory submission of the enemy to our will is the ultimate *object*" (p. 101). To be revolted by the nature of war, or to believe it should be moderated for moral reasons is absurd (p. 102). The "use of physical power to the utmost extent" (p. 102) will always triumph. "[I]t follows that he who uses force unsparingly, without reference to the bloodshed involved, must obtain a superiority if his adversary uses less vigour in its application" (p. 102). In the end, this remorseless and relentless will-to-violence is the essence of war. It is "the tendency to destroy the adversary which lies at the bottom of War [and] is in no way changed or modified through the progress of civilisation" (p. 103).

War is then a fit of passion that always remains in excess of diplomacy and politics. This passion is not, however, primeval violence, but merely an indication of the intensity of *interest*. Clausewitz writes,

> [W]hat a fallacy it would be to refer the War of a civilised nation entirely to an intelligent act on the part of the Government, and to imagine it as continually freeing itself more and more from all feeling of passion...If War is an *act* of force, it belongs necessarily also to the feelings, it *reacts* more or less, upon them, and the extent of this reaction depends not on the degree of civilisation, but on the importance and the duration of the interests involved.
> (1968, p. 103)

Passion in war springs from interest, but not the rational interest of calculated intention as much as the vehemence of unreflecting partisanship. Unshaped by the logic of policy imposed by politics and organised by genius, this passion becomes directed towards the annihilation of the enemy, and thus becomes identical with war in its ideal form. The stronger the interest, the more intense is the passion. The more intense the passion, the more war is war. Policy must play a double game. It must focus this passion in order to transform this, the most literally war of wars, into war as it should be, subordinate to the telos of policy:

> The greater and more powerful the motives of a War, the more it affects the whole existence of a people. The more violent the excitement which precedes the War, by so much nearer will the War approach to its abstract form, so much more will it be directed to the destruction of the enemy, so much nearer will the military and the political ends coincide, so much the more purely military and less political the War appears to be; but the weaker the motives and the tensions, so much less will the natural direction of the military element—that is, force—be coincident with the direction which the military element indicates; so much the more must, therefore, the War become diverted from its natural direction, the political object diverge from the aim of an ideal War, and the War appear to become political.
> (Clausewitz, 1968, pp. 119–20)

This passage comes immediately after the clearest formulation of the claim that war is mere policy. Here, the argument becomes more complicated. On the one hand, we have war in its ideal or natural form, a purely military phenomenon, fuelled by the interest and motivation of the people. On the other, we have the political. If the political is able to blend itself seamlessly with this military drive, then the war will not appear to be pure calculation and cold manipulation, but an outburst of collective passion. It will appear natural, uncontaminated by cynical power-play. If the passion is not strong, however, the natural war will weaken, and politics will appear in its loathsome nakedness.

There is a military nature, therefore, or a natural propensity to war, and it is here that we meet war in its abstract form, its essence. This is the war of force, passion, unconsidered interest and the people. Even the uncivilised primitives are capable of such a war. Clausewitz's aim, however, is to show that this war only makes sense when it has imposed upon it, or sown into it, the rational and civilised method of policy, which shapes interest into purpose, antipathy into ambition and war into meaning:

> Accordingly, War can never be separated from political intercourse, and if, in the consideration of the matter, this is done in any way, all the threads of the different relations are, to a certain extent, broken, and we have before us a senseless thing without an object.
> (Clausewitz, 1968, p. 402)

War can never be uncombined with political elements, as, in the end, the raw motivations of passion and the people are themselves albeit crude elements of the political anyway. War can never actually exist in its pure form, unshaped by policy. There is no degree zero of policy in war. It is always a "half-and-half thing, a contradiction in itself" (p. 403). For this reason, the idea of a war governed purely by hostility, a pure war is chimerical: war "cannot follow its own laws, but must be looked upon as a part of another whole—and this whole is policy" (p. 403).

War in Clausewitz is thus an unstable phenomenon: natural and popular energy and will-to-annihilation is war in its essence, but this essential war can never be without some political drive and is most successful and most useful, when the political element is perfectly co-ordinated with military energy. This co-ordination should be striven for, but is not guaranteed. This creates a contradiction in the nature of war between its two elements, its necessary military violence, and its irreducible connection with policy. This instability arises because neither of these elements can be reduced to zero. They are the map of an entire society. What links them and allows them to act is the charismatic figure of the military genius, only able to arise in the context of civilisation, and able, magically, from out of himself, to turn the infinity and obscurity of evaluation into knowable action, to which the chaotic natural force of the interest of the people can be attuned. The situation is delicate, however, and never guaranteed, and the balance between the military and the political remains always problematic.

In Clausewitz, then, there are two types of war: one, a war that follows the logic of violence to its end—"the rigorous law of forces exerted to the utmost" (Clausewitz, 1968, p. 108)—the other, the logic of policy that must be imposed on this war in order to make sense of it, and redeem it. The former of these two wars is the one he concedes, the latter the one he recommends. Even though his statements about war as policy are framed as if they are simply definitions of the nature of war as it is, it is clear that Clausewitz's project is to assert this understanding of rational war over alternatives. In this argument, rational purpose is not simply put forward as the true nature of war, it is recovered from wars that may appear on face value to be something else. Rational war supersedes what he calls variously "extreme," "absolute" or "ideal" war.

War is not simply instituted by policy as much as tamed by it, as some of his section headings indicate: "The probabilities of real life take the place of the conceptions of the extreme and the absolute" (Clausewitz, 1968, p. 108); "the political object now reappears" (p. 109). Policy is indeed "the original motive of the war" (p. 109), but it wrestles throughout with the tendency of war to the extreme. This tendency is identified with the people. A people must be constantly reminded of a war's political purpose, and have everything about the war, its experience and outcomes subordinated to that purpose:

> The political object, as the original motive of the War will be the standard for determining both the aim of the military force and also the amount and effort to be made...One and the same political object may produce totally different effects upon different people, or even upon the same people at different times; we can, therefore, only admit the political object as the measure, by considering it in its effects upon those masses which it is to move, and consequently the nature of those masses also comes into consideration. It is easy to see that thus the result may be very different according as these masses are animated with a spirit which will infuse vigour into the action or otherwise.
> (Clausewitz, 1968, p. 110)

The political object governs, therefore, both in theory and in practice, clarifying war and directing all its potentially chaotic energies in their unfolding.

What makes this account of war so important is that after the French Revolution, when war became a popular activity again, an "affair of the people" (Clausewitz, 1968, p. 384), war was now undertaken with such energy (p. 385) that the conventional logic of the aristocratic Art of War—dominant in the eighteenth century—was shattered. First on one side, and then the other and most completely under Bonaparte, the natural military energy identified with the essence of war came into its own. What happened was not the release of pointless violence but the identification of the people with the political, so that policy and energy became identified with one another. Here, when policy does not shape the will of the people but is that will, when war becomes an "affair of the whole Nation" (p. 386), war attains its ultimate form, its "ideal perfection" (p. 386).

War is thus always the activation of the society, by way of the uneasy and potentially contradictory match between the natural drive to violence and the descent of policy. If, however, policy and the people seem identified with one another, then war attains its ultimate form, and can generate an irresistible energy. It becomes the society in its total operation. *On War* is an unsettled text. There is, on the one hand, a war Clausewitz recognises, a "pure" or "ideal" war, one that he is wary of; on the other hand, there is a war he recommends, and there is the frightening unpredictable co-ordination of the two in the post-Revolutionary war of the whole Nation. This is not an account of war as the mere cool implementation of policy, though it can be represented as such. It is an account of war as a consequence of the social, either as élite policy or popular drive or the marriage between them.

In Hobbes and Kant, war is seen in different ways to be in contradiction with society. War is the thing that the institution of civil society and sovereign authority, on the one hand, or the fulfilment of duty, on the other, are intended either to escape or control. Yet, this means that war is always everywhere part of the definition of the social and political, and not merely by negative determination, whereby the social world is merely that which war is not. In Hobbes, civil society's purpose is to attain the goals of war that war itself is incapable of attaining. In Kant, war is the thing that allows peace to make sense. Only through war can peace be achieved.

In Clausewitz, war is not in contradiction with society. As the co-ordination of elite political intention and mass interest through the figure of the genius, war is society in action. Yet, the instability of the relationships here installs some volatility and tension at the heart of war.

These arguments plot the co-ordinates of the relationship between war and its other: Is war the opposite of society, or its simple enactment? These simple alternatives define the debate about the nature of war. Yet, at the same time, these writers also reveal the impossibility of keeping these arguments simple and resolute. The opposition between war and society ends by binding the two in an inextricable shared definition, which means that war is always and everywhere insistently present in the social. The idea of war as the continuity of the social actually ends by producing a riven and uneasy model of sociality. It is to attempts on the part of other writers to more resolutely negotiate these contradictions that we will now turn.

Part II
The War/Other Complex

So far we have seen accounts of war that present it as either the opposite to or a continuation of civil society. Ironically, we have seen how each of these accounts loses its clarity, and becomes something much less resolute: accounts of war as the opposite of civil society end by seeing the latter as either the fulfilment of war or only possible by way of it. Clausewitz's account of war as the enactment of civil society, far from producing a neat model of collective agency, presents the society that goes to war as complex and fraught, a combination of a partisan mass energy and élite calculation, mediated by the Romantic figure of the genius-general. These two versions of the relationship between war and its other remain definitive. As we will see, Clausewitz is referred to by almost every contemporary commentator on war, astonishingly almost always without much interrogation of his ideas, or even knowledge of their complexity. Similarly, we can see the Hobbesian inheritance in the mindless rush of policy makers and journalists to describe any fracture of the social consensus as a "war," specifically the implication that war is the horror that runs potentially unchecked beneath the fragile surface of all social relations, waiting for any opportunity to break through. Of course, in their pronouncements, we see not only a fear of, but a longing for war, at least as a moral abjection with which the conservative reflex can always reprove and threaten us.

The collapse of the definitiveness of these accounts of war is not as widely acknowledged as it has been richly theorised. War is a problem, but not only morally. What the accounts we have seen show is that it is not enough, or perhaps not even possible, to see war and its other as separate or identical, or, in any way, in a simple relationship with one another. War and its other contradict but also produce one another, but not simply by negatively determining one another. They produce one another in endless acts of mutual collaboration in which they remain hostile and threatening to one another. How are we to describe this irrational complex? This chapter aims to survey those thinkers from Freud to Derrida, who have tried to deal one way or another with this complexity. The aim will be to show that war and its other cannot be simply seen as either opposite to or continuous with one another. Instead, they incite, even require, one another while remaining threatening to one another. The values that sustain peaceful human interaction are both defended and advanced by war, even as war is the greatest threat to them. War pollutes and ruins the sociality it fights for. The challenge to the theorist is to go beyond the simple options outlined by Hobbes's and Clausewitz's positions in order to find some way of articulating this aporetic situation, which seems to defy logic. As we have seen, the positions of Hobbes and Clausewitz clearly point in this direction, because the situation they were attempting to describe was more volatile and complex than their conclusions would seem to indicate. As we mentioned in the Introduction, in a world in which doctrines of human rights have become the most articulate ways to both justify and critique war, this question of the double nature of the war/other relationship is more than an issue of theoretical interest, but a pressing global political problem.

Freud: War and ambivalence

The first thinker to argue for the double and ambiguous nature of war was Sigmund Freud, attempting to deal with his revulsion at the viciousness of the First World War. War interrupts Freud's thought with shock and disillusionment. How could a civilisation charged by history with the leadership of humanity succumb to an atavistic rampage of self-mutilating violence? How could psychoanalysis both understand this cataclysm and withstand it? Would the individualistic and intra-familial logic that had been the focus of the new science of psychoanalysis prove adequate to the task of explaining the formations of identity, subjectivity and aggression that produced war? Could psychoanalysis explain why the cosmopolitan Europe of Freud's dream of culture had so easily succumbed to, and so joyously embraced, a terror and violence that should have been long abandoned? Could we blame our ugly ancestors, long forgotten but somehow unburied in our turbulent psychology? Psychoanalysis responded to war in a variety of ways, ambitious to understand such an extreme and unexpected event, rethinking or re-emphasising certain core psychoanalytic ideas. The result was that the persistence of aggression, the charisma of death and the violence of authority would match desire, the erotic and love as fundamentals in the Freudian model of the human psyche, from now on. Indeed, Freud would come to argue that these things could never be seen as strictly separable from one another: love and aggression do not only accompany one another, but are part of a single complex, in which they cannot only foster but become one another. War confirms the fundamental ambivalence of all human relationships and identifications.

War for Freud is indeed a thing that lends itself to psychoanalytical explanation, even in its surprise and mystery. It can be isolated from the political and historical complexes—the alliances, institutions, opportunisms and miscalculations—out of which it emerges and that it helps compose, and be understood in its enduring conformity to some idea of generalised human psychology. The explanation for war is general, rather than specific, and is to do with the nature of human subjectivity. The causes of the present war are the cause of all wars, not the incidental logic of a specific event, nor the patterned unfolding of a complex of knowable and unknowable, contrived and recalled, installed and revealed, sometimes psychological, at others mass-political, democratic and animal, criminal and bureaucratic, masculine and feminine incidents that emerge and combine under the cover, in the name of or to pursue the purpose of war. Policy and banditry, tactic and sexual violence, diplomacy and atrocity: over and above the multitude of incidents and impulses that constitute it, to Freud, war is a discrete thing. It might have surprised us, but it is no more than a thing, and we can explain it in itself separate from the specific historical circumstances that give rise to it. All wars are the same in theory, and specific wars should not be mistaken for themselves. They are, in fact, an expression or realisation of collective human subjectivity. This is how psychoanalysis will explain war, and it is impatient to explain it, because it is not only equipped but duty-bound to understand, analyse and control any human thing whatsoever. This demystification remains psychoanalysis's mission, the patient undimming of the human even in its irretrievable darkness. Such knowledge may allow scientists to feel safe again, civilised once more, scientific still.

What does Freud say about war? Let us start with a look at his 1915 paper "Thoughts For the Times on War and Death." For Freud here, nothing has been more abused by war than thought itself. Under the present regime of war, everything is distorted, our perspective lacks distance and objectivity, the future is opaque. We are thinking and have ideas, but no ability to assess their quality. Even the science we have relied upon has been perverted in order to insult and abuse the enemy.

Anthropology and psychiatry have answered the trumpet call, and signed up to the national distemper. The depth of the crisis for science cannot be underestimated: science is used to malign your enemies. On the one hand, this confirms its authority. After all, who would care what science said if it had no authority? The very enlistment of science to the national cause is not science's defeat and subservience, but its apotheosis. People care enough what science says to use it to justify and rationalise their outrages. Yet, on the other hand, science is also squandering its authority, by displaying how easily impartiality, objectivity and rational conclusion can be faked. Science must emerge from this with something intact. Freud must protect science by allowing it to work through psychoanalysis. Through psychoanalysis's investigation of war itself, science can be seen to deal with, and thus to rise above, the very confusion that has compromised it.

In this way, psychoanalysis can be an exemplar of a socially responsible science. Freud's science does not function without its own commitment to social values, and those values are those that allowed science to arise: human inter-connectedness in its specifically European, cosmopolitan form. Science must necessarily emerge in some human context, especially a science like psychoanalysis, whose very means and material is human inter-subjectivity. The social value that has allowed psychoanalysis to emerge, that the war has disrupted, and for which Freud is in mourning, is the value that most facilitates the complex and insistent unfolding of human inter-connectedness in all its accident, plurality and largesse, the cosmopolitan, pan-European sense of Europe itself as summary, exemplum, fore-runner, *and* scientist of all the collectivities that compose the human. Psychoanalysis, therefore, is not merely a tool to be turned upon war, as readily as it can be turned on anything else, or as readily as any other methodology. It is already strongly positioned in relation to war. It has been made possible by the culture that withstood war for so long, and now it must recover that culture in order to imagine something that might survive the flames. What counts then is how previous reference-points in this culture have been affected—the sense of the continuity of cosmopolitan Europe, and the way war has reconfigured our relationship with death. The issue is not so much what war is in itself, but how to understand how "we" non-combatants feel (Freud, 1985, p. 62), in our disillusionment and in changed attitudes towards death. Psychoanalysis, and thus science in general, must show that they can endure war, analyse it, and make sense of it. War must not be beyond psychoanalysis. Psychoanalysis, developed through cosmopolitan civilisation, must be able to include, and thus over-reach, war.

Why are "we" so disillusioned? We knew that war was always possible, Freud argues, because of the irrepressible differences in the way people lived and in their different assessments of the value of human life. Wars between peoples of different coloured skin, between the civilised and primitive, even between people who have no civilisation (because they have not developed it or have lost it) could be expected, but a war between "the great world-dominating nations of white race upon whom the leadership of the human species has fallen" (Freud, 1985, p. 62) should have been unthinkable! It had seemed that so sympathetic were these nations to one another that national divisions were fading in the face of the development of "a new and wider fatherland" (p. 63) whose new citizenry could enjoy many and varied landscapes and wander in an open-ended museum of a shared and uplifting culture. "As he wandered from one gallery to another in this museum, he could recognise with impartial appreciation what varied types of perfection a mixture of blood, the course of history, and the special quality of their mother-earth has produced amongst his compatriots in the wider sense" (p. 63). It may be because of differences between human beings that we believed war was inevitable, but not this "variety" which is the animator of culture and science. Even war itself if it had to recur, between the civilised white races, would have been a civilised "chivalrous passage of arms" (p. 64), enduring only as long as necessary to establish who was superior in strength alone.

Instead of this difference based on commonality through admixture leading to civilised because measured and purposeful war, what has arisen is a war "as cruel, as embittered, as implacable as any that has preceded it" (p. 65), one not only vicious in its unfolding drama, but enduringly cataclysmic in what Freud intuits to be its destiny, which seems to be the destruction of the apparently fragile networks of civility and shared civilisation in which he thought he had been living. "It cuts all bonds between the contending peoples, and threatens to leave a legacy of embitterment that will make any renewal of those bonds impossible for a long time to come" (p. 65).

The civilisation that has been lost relied on the repression of "instinctual satisfaction" (p. 62) at great expense to the individual. Now, the society itself, in its executive arm, the State, does not enforce that repression on itself, engaging in all styles of viciousness and deceit, a lapse that has consequences for the self-restraint of individuals as well (p. 66). Since the origin of self-restraint is "'social anxiety' and nothing else," (p. 66) then "men [will] perpetrate deeds of cruelty, fraud, treachery and barbarity so incompatible with their level of civilisation that one would have thought them impossible" (p. 67). Repression, the lodestone and guarantee of the quality of human inter-relations has itself been put at risk.

Yet "our" surprise is not a simple reaction to the unforeseen. It merely shows how deluded "we" were. Surprise—were "we" (who?) really surprised outside of Freud's rhetorical figuring? who was surprised and in what way?—shows a fundamental misunderstanding of human psychology. Human beings, according to Freud, attribute virtue either to an innate quality of "the soul" (something so unscientific and inarticulable that Freud will ignore it) or to the socialising processes that have been "eradicating [the individual's] evil human tendencies and, under the influence of education and a civilised environment, replacing them by good ones" (p. 67). Yet psychoanalysis shows that human beings are motivated by "instinctual impulses which are of an elementary nature" (p. 68) that are not subject to a simple moral evaluation except in specific social contexts. These drives may be complicated, redirected or even pluralised by social influences. Most interestingly and importantly, as we shall see, an ambivalence may emerge from a simple object-relation. Intense love and hatred may be manifest towards the same object. Bad—here understood as egoistic—impulses may be transformed into good by the influence of the erotic instincts that promote sociality. We value being loved and this social validation of the ego wins out over more solipsistic egotism. Externally derived validation of the ego not only overwhelms any confirmation of the self derived from within, but replaces it, till the subject internalises society's values: "[t]he influences of civilisation cause an ever-increasing transformation of egoistic trends into altruistic and social ones by an admixture of erotic elements" (p. 69). In fact, the internal impulses in the subject were originally externally derived. In the modern subject, this external derivation of the sense of self is strengthened by an inheritance from ancestors: "Those who are born today bring with them as an inherited organisation some degree of tendency (disposition) towards the transformation of egoistic into social instincts, and this disposition is easily stimulated into bringing about that result" (p. 69).

This disposition towards pro-social behaviour is drawn on by society through a pattern of rewards and punishments which is so successful that it fools us into believing that human beings are essentially or substantially better than they really are. Yet, in the economy of subjectivity, this pressure gives rise to an inevitable reaction. The "pressure of civilisation brings in its train no pathological results... but is shown in malformations of character, and in the perpetual readiness of the inhibited instincts to break through to satisfaction at any suitable opportunity" (Freud, 1985, p. 71). As a consequence, we are living psychologically "beyond [our] means" (p. 72), and although civilisation itself may depend on it, such a delicate balance is unsustainable.

So the disillusionment "we" may have suffered because of this war was unjustified because we should never have expected any better from our fellow human beings: "In reality our fellow-citizens have not sunk so low as we feared, because they had never risen so high as we believed" (Freud, 1985, p. 72). The fact that societies and nation states had themselves abandoned their own standards of legality and civility licensed individuals to "grant a temporary satisfaction to the instincts which they had been holding in check" (p. 72). In Freud's account, the violence that individuals enact in war is the result of a buried and indirect social pressure: it is not the result of the many other factors that could explain the violence of soldiers, such as the compulsion to enlist, the discipline of the armed forces, the incontrovertibility of orders, a loyalty to the society or nation as an idea, the need to protect loved ones, the determination to defend fellow troops in a dangerous situation or fear of the punishment threatened for disobedience or desertion. Military action is not a manifestation of social order and repression, according to Freud in this essay, but an example of their failure. Freud takes for granted that there is not only some psychic satisfaction in war, but some orgiastic enthusiasm for it, and that it is this that needs explaining. That in some situations, even in some cultures, perhaps our own, it may be repression itself and not its release that manifests itself in violence or even orgy, and atrocity is not seriously considered. There is an opposition between violence and passion, on the one hand, and repression and sociality, on the other. Later, as we will see in Freud's discussion of the relationship between the individual soldier, group identity and the leader, motivation will take on other forms.

The civilisation of the scientist, then, is on the side of repression, and recognises repression's other, egoistic violence, as its antagonist unleashed by war. So far then the disposition human beings have inherited from their forebears has been oriented towards civilisation and repression. Now, however, Freud will present the mind as loaded with another type of inheritance altogether. The relation between these inheritances is not fully clear, but it seems the mind has a "special capacity for...regression" (Freud, 1985, p. 73). The "higher" stages of human development may be lost if one slips back, but the "primitive stages can always be re-established; the primitive mind is, in the fullest meaning of the word, imperishable" (p. 73). Mental illness itself can be attributed to this weakening of the higher stages of mental development and the concomitant "return to earlier stages of affective life and of functioning" (p. 73).

War then is a psychological more than a political or historical event. It represents a loosening of the repressive bonds of civilisation, but is a consequence of their previous strictness. We have been repressed in the past in order to enter into civil society, and this has built up a pressure awaiting release. The eschewing of moral restraint on the part of the State tells us it is acceptable for individuals to throw off the burden of repression, and release primitive energies, which have not only been controlled by the social instinct, but intensified by their pressure. War is an anti-social act. It is hostile to civilisation. Yet, since war is implicitly a counter to the intensity of repression, it is a necessary and inalienable part of its economy, and thus of the logic of civilisation itself. War opposes, undermines and reacts against civilisation as a part of the processes by which civilisation becomes possible. War is inevitably produced as a consequence of, and counter-movement to, the repression of violence that initiated civilisation. Civilisation and violence, therefore, are not opposites or alien qualities, but necessarily inter-related parts of a single economy. They contradict yet cause one another, and can never be absolutely separate from one another.

Despite the vastly different discourses that define their separate trajectories—the legal-political, on the one hand, and subjective-energetic, on the other—both Hobbes and Freud imagine a mythical primitive past of necessary violence, and a present social order permanently entailed to it because social order's primary reason for being is always to save us from, even *redeem*, our violence. In the very process by which war is alienated, it is made the permanent if unhappy partner and the very meaning of civil society, a perpetual threat in Hobbes, always inevitably to return, according to Freud. These primeval people, our ancestors, have never actually existed, according to Freud, and are a mere construct of speculation (as he admits: Freud, 1985, p. 80). Their role is to be the same as us: they "certainly" have the same attitude towards death and "undoubtedly" their loved ones (p. 81), but they are also simpler, starker and more passionate. They substantiate our nature by providing it with a long history. In short, our present feelings are not created by war, but merely revealed, animated or released by it. Freud subordinates war to the logic of human psychology. War is not an interruption, distortion or radical recreation of human emotion, but a dramatisation of it. As Freud mentioned from the outset, war has instilled an intense discomfort in those who have been left behind, those cosmopolitan intellectuals who have seen their prized pan-European culture perverted. Fighting back requires an objective address to war. Victory over war involves assimilating it to what psychoanalysis already knows. The status of cosmopolitan culture has to be guaranteed by proof that it is larger than war. Theory must secure the ultimate victory by not only knowing war, but by knowing it as subordinate to theoretical logic. Reduced only to the bearer of violence, primeval man and his own complex feelings never emerge in any specificity in Freud's discourse, but only as the prototype and guarantee of the nature of a not necessarily so thoroughly modern "us:" "The man of prehistoric times survives unchanged in our unconscious" (Freud, 1985, p. 85). Primeval man is our secret but animating truth. We are as vicious and violent as he was. The intensity of our ethical codes proves it. We would not need such strong prohibitions against killing if we did not have a strong impulse towards it.

War reveals the ambiguity of civilisation, its inevitable entanglement with violence. It also makes obvious our ambivalent attitudes towards death. If the war has succeeded in complicating Freud's view of a consensual and harmonious white European civilisation, it has made death seem only more real. "Death will no longer be denied," Freud writes, "we are forced to believe in it...Life has, indeed, become interesting again; it has recovered its full content" (Freud, 1985, pp. 79–80). War has forced us to abandon our conventional culture of death without us yet having contrived a replacement for it. Freud ponders the way of death of "primeval man." Death was, according to Freud's speculation, both something more immediately real to primitive people, and something to be abstracted by, for example, the transformation of those he had murdered into both objects of worship and the source of an inheritable sense of guilt, as had already been argued in *Totem and Taboo* (1912–13).

The death of loved ones was an intense process, because it revealed beneath intimacy an unrecognised sense of estrangement and hostility. This imaginary primeval man felt a great sorrow at the death of loved ones, but also a secret irrepressible pleasure:

> The law of ambivalence of feeling, which to this day governs our emotional relations with those whom we love most, certainly had a very much wider validity in primeval times. Thus those beloved dead had also been enemies and strangers who had aroused in him some degree of hostile feeling.
>
> (Freud, 1985, p. 82)

Even our most loyal and pure loves are polluted by a trace of hatred. This complexity even refreshes our love and makes it more intense: "It might be said that we owe the fairest flowerings of our love to the reaction against the hostile impulse which we sense within us" (p. 88). How does such a statement help us cope with war? Here, the unity of Freud's argument in this paper becomes apparent. We have the answer here to the painful question which dominates the first section of this essay. How could the borderless, cosmopolitan culture that had supposedly made Europe the leader of humanity, the playground of the educated tourist and the museum of higher sensibility, have given way to vicious and abusive internecine violence? The answer is that, in exactly the same way that civilisation always carries with it a trace of war, indeed provoking it and reanimating it inevitably, love always carries with it a trace of hostility. War is not simply the result of human differences. There are different differences. There is the difference across which human beings cannot recognise each other and there is the difference of the cosmopolitan plurality that had allowed sciences like psychoanalysis to flourish. The former explains the wars of the unfinished cultures of the not-yet-advanced, and the wars that "civilised" societies might wage against them. The wars of the cosmopolitan nations, on the other hand, are wars where an apparent bond, indeed a familial love, had within it a hostility that in the end cannot be absolutely surpassed, and that must always be reawakened. War is part of the economy of love. In short, to Freud, there are two kinds of wars: on the one hand, there are what we might call colonial wars, wars between more and less advanced societies, or between human groups that have not advanced to the complex kinds of bonds that unite human communities. On the other hand, there are civil wars. The former are inevitable and to be expected. The latter are shocking and disillusioning, because they have pitted what "we" thought of as "us" against ourselves. These are wars of love, therefore, in which our complex and ambivalent attitude towards those with whom we bond and identify releases its underside: antagonism, resentment and vindictiveness.

Repression and love have made us what we are: civilised, communal, affirming of the social bond. Yet they carry within them a hostility that they must, in the end, either lapse into or provoke. In the end, we must accept this complexity and expect it. Jacqueline Rose says, "Guilt projection is...the driving force of cultural humanization *and* the basis of the destruction of all culture. It is incapable as a concept of distinguishing between socially desirable and socially undesirable effects" (Rose, 1993, p. 31). Psychoanalysis cannot settle for the humanist truism which argues that war is simply primitive and anti-cultural, nor the one that culture is always unambiguously good. Freud intuited that the guilt projection which defined the ambiguity of the subject's orientation to the (love-) object entangles our relationships in an economy of forces that cannot be easily made to resolve into simple preferences. War emerges from beneath love; cosmopolitanism belies antagonism; science legitimises warfare. Violence and hatred are not things that attack and undermine love from the outside. They are a necessary part of the definition of love itself.

Freud discusses the management of primitive aggression in *Civilisation and Its Discontents*. He alludes to the violence and atrocities of the Mongol invasions, the Crusades and the "recent world war," then writes,

> The existence of this inclination to aggression, which we can detect in ourselves and justly assume to be present in others, is the factor which disturbs our neighbour and which forces civilisation into such a high expenditure [of energy]. In consequence of this primary mutual hostility of human beings, civilised society is perpetually threatened with disintegration. The interest of work in common would not hold it together; instinctual passions are stronger than reasonable interests. Civilisation has to use its utmost efforts in order to set limits to man's aggressive instincts and to hold the manifestations of them in check by psychical reaction-formations. Hence, therefore, the use of methods intended to incite people into identifications and aim-inhibited relationships of love, hence the restriction upon sexual life, and hence too the ideal's commandment to love one's neighbour as oneself—a commandment which is really justified by the fact that nothing else runs so strongly counter to the original nature of man. In spite of every effort, these endeavours of civilisation have not so far achieved very much. It hopes to prevent the crudest excesses of brutal violence by itself assuming the right to use violence against criminals, but the law is not able to lay hold of the more cautious and refined manifestations of human aggressiveness. The time comes when each one of us has to give up as illusions the expectations which, in his youth, he pinned upon his fellow-men, and when he may learn how much difficulty and pain has been added to his life by their ill-will. At the same time, it would be unfair to reproach civilisation with trying to eliminate strife and competition from human activity. These things are undoubtedly indispensable.
>
> (Freud, 1985, pp. 302–3)

The economic cost to our civilisation of our inherited and primary inclination to aggression is immense. Much energy is required to manage it. The solution is seen in the education of individuals into pro-social "relationships of love," but ones in which the drive to satisfaction is somehow inhibited. Yet, as we will see, the erotic bond that ties us together into groups is also tangled up with the impulse towards violence. In sum, not only is violence part of the relationships we—or the groups we belong to—have with others, it is also a part of what constitutes all human subjectivity, both individual and collective.

The complex relationship between love and war is discussed further in Freud's paper on group psychology. Here, military organisation proves also to be a version of love. This is because armies and other military formations are clear examples of the logic of the human group, which all must be understood as enactments of a type of love. "We will try our fortune, then," says Freud, "with the supposition that love relationships... also constitute the essence of the group mind" (Freud, 1985, p. 120). Groups form because of some kind of binding force. Since love is the Freudian term for sociality, and combination, in general, then it is to love that we must look for an explanation of group psychology.

Freud looks to two examples of institutions where a group mentality is indispensable: the Church and the army. What is crucial—and what earlier thinkers of the group have overlooked—is the focus of these institutions around the figure of the leader (Freud, 1985, p. 123) or at least the "leading idea" (p. 124). If we seek to understand the relationship with the leader that subordinates the subject to the logic of the group, then it is by way of love that we must proceed. When we are in love, according to Freud, "a considerable amount of narcissistic libido overflows onto the object" (p. 143) causing us to overvalue the person we are in love with. Yet, the status of our lover is not to do with their qualities as a person, but develops because they have become "a substitute for some unattained ego ideal of our own" (p. 143). We are unable to live out these ideals ourselves, and fall in love as a way of confirming that this idealised self is actually achievable, if not in ourselves, then at least in another person. A group forms when a number of individuals adopt a specific object—the leader—"in the place of their ego ideal" (p. 147). This identification produces a commonality amongst group members at the level of the ego. Because they share the love object, they come to identify with one another.

Again the primitive is evoked as a way of confirming this model of the group, and in order to show how long it has endured. The group is a "revival of the primal horde" (Freud, 1985, p. 155), in which the universal and equalising fear and paranoia directed towards the primal father is replaced by "the illusion that the leader loves all the individuals equally and justly" (p. 157). Fear and persecution also perform a binding function in the persistent sense of danger and violence—of authority and discipline—within the group, but they too are now to be understood as versions of love in the economy of love and hate. "What is thus awakened is the idea of a paramount and dangerous personality, towards whom only a passive-masochistic attitude is possible, to whom one's will has to be surrendered" (p. 160). The group with its subtle powers of coercive suggestion "still wishes to be governed by unrestricted force; it has an extreme passion for authority...a thirst for obedience" (p. 160). The ego-ideal that governs the ego is now explicitly outside of the subject, and the power of suggestion—the perceptions and ideas circulating within the group, validated by its relationships, especially with the leader, and constituting its culture—mediates the individual's relationship with reality. This means that the individual's perception of reality is both facilitated and distorted by the "erotic tie" (p. 160) of the group.

The army then, as an example of this group psychology, institutionalises ambivalence. It gives structure to an erotic solidarity analogous to sexual love, in the cult of the leader that is indispensable to, even definitive of, the group. This love bears with it the legacy of the primitive relationship with the primal father, whose murder inaugurates society, and the culture of guilt it causes, out of which have sprung religion and morality. The relationship with the leader, then, combines love, identification and desire, on the one hand, and aggression, fear and violence, on the other. Duty and obligation must combine these contradictory feelings. The social bond both requires and forbids aggression. The aim of social groups is to manage and exclude violence while also reserving violence for their own ends. In the case of the military, the complexity here becomes particularly acute, something perhaps only half-recognised by Freud. The army is a group built on a love relationship. Whatever aggression persists within the group must be controlled to stop it from disintegrating, and to allow it to remain as a functioning unit. Yet, at the same time, its very reason for being is to execute the most purposeful and elaborate violence, to perfect a destruction to which no other human activity can remotely compare.

The complication is that both the aggression within the army, felt towards the leader as the feared refiguring of the primal father, and the hatred, felt towards the enemy, bear within them a trace of the love inherent in all objectification. As we have seen, the army exists in a complex economy of love and hate, as required by its need in warfare for an object of hostility, and in its own institution, of a process of identification which makes solidarity, hierarchy and discipline possible. This ambivalence is merely a microcosm of its similarly complex relationship with humanity and civilisation in which it both expresses aggression and frustrates it. It exists in order to postpone and frustrate the violence that is essential to it, and that it must enact. In this sense, it is analogous to sexual love, which is intensified and perpetuated by delay and inhibition. The consequences of this tangled economy are significant. Because it aims to control and encourage by a complex inhibition and incitement, warfare cannot ever absolutely avoid the logic of atrocity and uncontrolled violence. The army is a controlled violence formation. The repression of violence that it manifests in the logic of the group formation has as its aim not the simple perpetuation of the erotic bond that binds all things together. Its aim is to repress violence in order to make it all the more effective elsewhere. This pattern of inhibition and expression enlists within it a logic of release and abandonment that cannot be kept clearly separate from a will-to-excess, and that may even be experienced as a kind of apotheosis of the group's own logic, or glory. In other words, atrocity is inalienable from the army. Its complex imbrication with love, and in turn, the sexualisation of love in Freud and the Freudian legacy, means that the violence that leads to atrocity will always be at least notionally sexualised.

The second consequence is for Freud's theory of the group. The group may exist as a way of controlling violence and aggression, but will always require them as well. It therefore becomes impossible to imagine civilisation succeeding in its necessary, if naïve mission. In the end, we must resign ourselves to civilisation's failure, the undiminishing resentment and malice of our fellow human beings and a concomitant disillusionment, as Freud does here. The disillusionment betokens not defeat, however, as much as a recognition of the complex economy in which aggressiveness reveals itself. Aggressiveness, Freud writes, "forms the basis of every relation of affection and love among people" (p. 304).

In *Civilisation and Its Discontents*, Freud develops this theme in a discussion of the formation of the superego, and the nature of the human conscience. The superego explains how civilisation keeps a check on the aggressiveness of the individual. The prohibition directed against aggression can only be maintained if it is internalised, and becomes directed towards the ego (Freud, 1985, p. 315). The ego becomes divided, a portion of it sets itself over the rest, and the superego is formed.

The superego is the representative of civilisation in the subject. Freud compares it to a garrison overseeing a conquered town (p. 316). The superego is not simply proportionate to what is required, however. It may help civilisation by controlling the subject's drive to aggression, but it overdoes it, looking for ways of getting the ego punished (p. 318). The ego, therefore, is subjected to the superego's insatiable drive to condemn it, and seeks endlessly for its approval, but in vain. There are thus two stages in the development of conscience: first, the formation of the superego as an internalisation of a feared authority, and secondly the directing of fear at the superego itself. The first inaugurates the regime that controls, amongst other things, the aggressive instincts. The second responds to the fact that this control can never be fully successful, and seeks punishment for the incurable ego (Freud, 1985, p. 319). What motivated the original renunciation of aggression, therefore, was the need to preserve the relationship with an external authority. The subject fears the loss of this authority's love. In the next stage, the subject is aware that the renunciation of the instincts has been imperfect, and the drive to aggression persists, even if it is never acted upon. In this way, the subject has no protection from the surveillance of the superego, and a sense of guilt arises (p. 320). The consequences of this for the subject are unhappy. At least, when it was imagined that there was an external judge that the subject could potentially placate by its acts of renunciation, there was some possibility of pleasing authority, gaining approval and being at psychological peace. But, with the superego, there is no manifest measure of adequacy in renunciation. There is no external measure or reward for virtue. The subject is locked in a "permanent internal unhappiness...the tension of the sense of guilt" (Freud, 1985, p. 320).

But Freud is not satisfied with this explanation for the origin of conscience, particularly in relation to the question of why the most virtuous people have the most intractable consciences. His answer is that conscience does not simply arise because of the internalisation of disapproval of aggression. Conscience pre-existed aggression and leads to its renunciation in the first place. The result of this is an ever-intensifying economic cycle in which conscience leads to the renunciation of aggression that in turn strengthens the conscience, and so on. But where did this initial conscience come from, if so far, the explanation for conscience has been that it is a consequence of the internalisation of the loved authority figure that demanded renunciation in the first place? How can this primal figure pre-exist itself? Freud's answer is that the child does not only feel an aggressiveness that the authority figure seeks to have renounced. The demand that renunciation takes place itself provokes aggressiveness in the child, but towards the authority figure itself, in anger for the demand it places on the child to renounce its deepest drives. The child identifies with the authority figure, who then becomes a version of his ego, but the authority also is internalised as the superego, now in possession of all the aggressiveness the child originally felt towards the figure who sought for him to renounce his aggression in the first place. The severity of the superego's relationship to the ego, then, originates not in the authority's manifest disapproval of the subject's aggressiveness, but in the aggressiveness felt by the subject towards the authority. Conscience is not first formed then by a reaction to the renunciation of aggression, but a resentment towards the figure who commands the renunciation. The subject seeks to punish an internalised version of this figure because the demand to renounce angers him.

Thus conscience pre-exists the renunciation of aggression, even though it is continually intensified by it. What this allows Freud to explain is why, in *Totem and Taboo*, the brothers who banded together to murder the primal father felt remorse at what they had done. They gave in to their feeling of aggression towards their cruel and terrible patriarch, but this anger did not exhaust their feelings towards him. They identified with and loved him as well:

> After their hatred had been satisfied by their act of aggression, their love came to the fore in their remorse for the deed. It set up the superego by identification with the father; it gave that agency the father's power, as though as a punishment for the deed of aggression they had carried out against him, and it created the restrictions which were intended to prevent a repetition of the deed.
>
> (Freud, 1985, p. 325)

The primal father then controls the sons' aggressiveness. They feel aggression towards him because of this, a drama which they internalise in their identification with him. Their ambivalence towards him— they identify with him but feel aggression towards him—results both in aggression manifest towards him and in remorse at this same aggression.

In the army, as we have already seen, the primal father is the prototype of the leader on whose love the members of the group focus. The soldier seeks to obey the leader by taking on a passive-masochistic attitude towards him. At the same time, the leader is a love-object for the soldier and thus a version of his ego-ideal. Again, we find the complex relationship in which love and aggression are entangled. The soldier submits to the leader whom he thinks of as an ideal version of himself, and thus an object of love. But, if he is a version of the primal father, then he also resents his need to control his aggression. In turn, the leader's attempts to control the soldier's aggression provoke aggression towards the leader, which both allows and complicates the soldier's self-discipline. The soldier controls his aggression by the installation into himself of the leader's commandment that he renounce his aggression, but this only makes his aggression all the more intense. The soldier's aggression is surrendered to the leader, while at the same time breaking free of the leader, becoming secret and being directed against the figure of the leader within the soldier's subjectivity.

Obedience to the father/leader then both promotes the soldier's aggressiveness and robs him of it. His freedom of aggression is his dirty torturous secret, while his controlled aggression is the property of the leader. In other words, the more the leader seeks to marshal the aggressiveness of the soldier, the more he provokes it somewhere else as a guilty and poisonous love. The soldier's violence is taken away from him, while it is intensified within in the form of restraint and discipline. This discipline is experienced as a kind of masochistic love. On the side of the leader then we have an arrogation and appropriation of aggressiveness. On the part of the soldier, we have a loss of a right to private aggressiveness at the same time as that aggressiveness, in the form of a violent and antipathetic love towards the leader, is being promoted in the very mechanism of the discipline the leader is attempting to instil. Then, in a complex Freud did not really seem to contemplate, the violence the leader has appropriated is unleashed again on some selected object, but *through* the soldier. The soldier's aggressiveness has been appropriated by the leader, but is then sent back from the leader through the soldier. The aggression that the soldier feels towards the leader that has become military discipline in the form of the soldierly conscience combines with this reproressed primal aggression and seeks an object to love. The soldier loves violently, kills passionately, protects viciously, honours cruelly, obeys angrily, fights for peace, is loyal defiantly, defends what society values and then is abandoned.

So far, we have seen how war enacts ambivalence in two ways in Freud: first, by revealing that human relationships always combine violence and aggression with love, and secondly, in the structure of the army, where a complex economy of identification and love, on the one hand, and antipathy and obligation, on the other, produce a highly charged institution, which cultivates love and aggression simultaneously and in the one place, an economy that risks uncontrollable violence, indeed a violence we cannot bear to acknowledge, loaded with love. If we attempt to summarise the Freudian account of war, we see a complex economy of love and aggression. This involves shifting identifications and relationships between the soldier-subject, the leader, the community, the enemy, the social in general, and Eros and Thanatos, life and death. For example, the leader both forbids and demands the soldier's aggression, while remaining himself an object of both a love and a hostility that the soldier internalises and reproduces as a version of the shifting, reversible relationship between his ego and his superego. War requires aggressiveness on the part of soldiers, of course, but an aggressiveness that is controlled, precisely targeted, even fierce, but not random, personal or spontaneous. Freud reveals that this aggressiveness will always contain within it the seeds of a resistance to it (in the form of refusal or mutiny), the possibility of the self-mutilation of the soldier and the risk of excess and atrocity. These military heresies are not accidents that strike military culture from the outside, but are, to the Freudian reading, inevitably part of the economy of warfare, even as it tries to control them. The economy of love and aggression makes atrocity inevitable. The complex involvement of Eros here also gives military violence an inherently sexual connotation, which emerges in the use of rape as a weapon.

In Section VI of *Civilisation and Its Discontents*, Freud generalises the relationship between love and aggressiveness under civilisation, revealing the impact the First World War has had on his thought. He traces the development of his thinking on this topic from the idea that human life is defined by twin drives, one towards the "preservation of the individual" (Freud, 1985, p. 308) or ego-instincts, and the other towards love, or the drive to the "preservation of the species," which becomes generalised as "object-instincts" (p. 308). It was clear, however, from the example of sadism that object-instincts were not always loving, even though they were demonstrably sexual. This conundrum was explained by the idea that sadism was merely a type of love in every way, except that "affection [is] replaced by cruelty" (p. 309). The break-through in thinking on this paradox came with the theory of narcissism, developed in the article of 1914, where the polarity between ego-instincts and object-choices was questioned. Narcissism represented "the discovery that the ego itself is cathected with libido, that the ego, indeed, is the libido's original home, and remains to some extent its headquarters. This narcissistic libido turns towards objects, and thus becomes object-libido; and it can change back into narcissistic libido once more" (p. 309). The relationship to the object is a displacement of libidinal investment in the ego, which will in turn rediscover the ego as its object. Ego-instincts and object-cathexes, then, flow into, substitute for and contradict one another, while remaining in uninterrupted relation.

The next major step was in *Beyond the Pleasure Principle* (1920). Although war does not play a major explicit role in the unfolding of this paper, it haunts it. The fort/da anecdote, for example, refers to the absence of the child's father at the front, and its preoccupation with death and aggressiveness takes up themes from the earlier war essay. The death-instinct emerges as a concept, therefore, against the background of war. In *Beyond the Pleasure Principle*, life is seen as the interplay and conflict between Eros and Thanatos, the instinct to life and the death-instinct. The death-instinct, however, was less visible than its counterpart. Freud interpreted this in the light of the argument on narcissism that "a portion of the [death-]instinct is diverted towards the external world and comes to light as an instinct of aggressiveness and destructiveness" (Freud, 1985, p. 310). It could even be argued that this projection outwards of the death-instinct served Eros "in that the organism was destroying some other thing, whether animate or inanimate, instead of destroying its own self" (p. 310).

The summation, then, of the relationship between Eros and Thanatos is that the instincts towards life and towards death always operate together, "that the two kinds of instinct seldom—perhaps never—appear in isolation from each other, but are alloyed with each other in varying and very different proportions and so become unrecognisable to our judgement" (p. 310). In fact, it is Eros that allows the aggressive instinct to become visible, especially in sadism, which is Freud's general term for the will to dominance:

> It is in sadism, where the death instinct twists the erotic aim in its own sense and yet at the same time fully satisfies the erotic urge, that we succeed in obtaining the clearest insight into its own nature and its relation to Eros. But even where it emerges without any sexual purpose, in the blind fury of destructiveness, we cannot fail to recognise that the satisfaction of the instinct is accompanied by an extraordinarily high degree of narcissistic enjoyment, owing to its presenting the ego with a fulfilment of the latter's old wishes for omnipotence. The instinct of destruction, moderated and tamed, and, as it were, inhibited in its aim, must, when it is directed towards objects, provide the ego with the satisfaction of its vital needs and with control over nature.
> (Freud, 1985, p. 313)

Here, control over nature is presented as a managed application of the aggressiveness of the death-instinct, operating in its inextricable, economic relationship with Eros. Earlier, control over nature was presented as the most progressive and sociable fruit of human community: the external world could be dealt with via "another and better path: that of becoming a member of the human community, and, with the help of a technique guided by science, going over to the attack against nature and subjecting her to the human will. Then one is working with all for the good of all" (Freud, 1985, p. 265). Now, control of nature emerges from the death-instinct, the subversive twin of Eros.

Does Freud think human power over nature is the result of civilisation and sociality or of a narcissistic aggressiveness somehow tempered by Eros? This question is not easy to answer. What it is important to recognise here is the complexity of the model Freud is trying to develop and his ethical difficulty with it. Together Eros and aggressiveness share "world-dominion" (p. 314). The development of humanity is the contest between these two instincts in their mutual imbrication. Eros and Thanatos often work together, and even seem to disappear behind or into one another. They can even transmute into one another, and must. Yet their relationship is complex and fraught with competition, contradiction and mutual challenge. Their co-ordination should not be seen as a simple machine whose working parts engage, assist and further one another. They remain distinct and are in irreducible contradiction with one another. Civilisation in Freud's mind is both the service of Eros and

> the struggle between Eros and Death, between the instinct of life and the instinct of destruction, as it works itself out in the human species. This struggle is what all life essentially consists of, and the evolution of civilisation may therefore be simply described as the struggle for life of the human species.
>
> (Freud, 1985, p. 314)

Now, Freud claims, "the meaning of the evolution of civilisation is no longer obscure to us" (p. 314). Yet, there is an uncontrolled shifting here. Civilisation represents the mission of Eros, but it also represents an undiminished and interminable struggle. Freud wants to present the relationship between Eros and Thanatos in its full economy, where the two are inseparable, mutually supportive and constitutive even in their challenge to and drive to subvert and frustrate one another. Yet, he also wants to retrieve some ethical preference from this complex by weighting the scales of civilisation in Eros' and thus sociality's favour.

War and love then are in an inextricably complex economic relation, but one in which choices and weightings must be made. It is a mistake to believe that these ethical considerations can be seen to be embedded in the system, where certain moral priorities are seen to be on the side of life itself. Yet, the relationship between Eros and Thanatos cannot be simply balanced so we see them as equally acceptable and arguable alternatives. Their very economic instability means there will always be a disproportion and conflict between them that can never settle into stasis and license a simple relativism.

War has now become normalised, for Freud. It is now an inevitable part of human sociality, no longer an enigma, arising to surprise us, and unsettle the patient evolution of science and civilisation. When Einstein asks him: "Is there any way of delivering mankind from the menace of war?" (Freud, 1985, p. 345), Freud's response is to challenge the polarity between violence and the right: "To-day right and violence appear to us as antitheses. It can easily be shown, however, that the one has developed out of the other" (p. 350). Freud argues that in the climate of primitive violence, the weak combined into a community that legitimated itself by instituting the law (p. 351).

> Thus we see that right is the might of a community. It is still violence, ready to be directed against any individual who resists it...The recognition of a community of interests such as these leads to the growth of emotional ties between the members of a united group of people—communal feelings which are the true source of its strength.
> (p. 351)

Here, the generalised tie that binds human society together arises not from an innate erotic drive, but through the practical necessity of managing violence.

Inside the community, however, differences remain that cause a social hierarchy to arise. Those who come to dominate threaten the communal bond of right by reverting to violence as a way of ensuring their own domination, and others jockey to gain power for themselves. This can lead to unrest, revolution and the overturning of the law and an establishment of a new regime of right. "Thus we see that the violent solution of conflicts of interest is not avoided even inside a community" (Freud, 1985, p. 353). Here we seem to have a practical historical account of the relationship between Eros and violence. Again, they are in an inextricable and necessarily economic relationship, but this has developed largely pragmatically, as a way of dealing with certain problems whose origins are outside of this relationship: social power and control over property.

However, Freud does connect these pragmatic political situations with the psychoanalytic theory of war he has already developed. He describes for Einstein the psychoanalytic theory of the innate relationship between Eros and aggressiveness. We have already seen this argument: there are instincts which seek to "preserve and unite" and those which seek to "destroy and kill" (Freud, 1985, p. 356). What is important for Freud is to see these twin impulses in their complicated operation:

> Neither of these instincts is any less essential than the other; the phenomena of life arise from the concurrent or mutually opposing actions of both. Now it seems as though an instinct of the one sort can scarcely ever operate in isolation; it is always accompanied—or, as we say, alloyed—with a certain quota from the other side, which modifies its aim or is, in some cases, what enables it to achieve that aim. Thus, for instance, the instinct of self-preservation is certainly of an erotic kind, but it must nevertheless have aggressiveness at its disposal if it is to fulfil its purpose. So, too, the instinct of love, when it is directed towards an object, stands in need of some contribution from the instinct for mastery if it is in any way to gain possession of that object. The difficulty of isolating the two classes of instinct in their actual manifestations is indeed what has so long prevented us from recognizing them.
> (Freud, 1985, p. 356)

This already complex and fluid situation is that no human action should be seen as simply the result of a single impulse, even if it is already accepted that that impulse itself is the combination of both Eros and aggressiveness. People may fight wars for a variety of reasons then, and because of a complex combination of idealistic and base motives. In atrocity, for example, idealistic motives may be merely a cover for aggressiveness or, as in the case of the Inquisition, "idealistic motives pushed themselves forward in consciousness, while the destructive ones lent them an unconscious reinforcement" (Freud, 1985, p. 357).

The death instinct, as we can recall from *Beyond the Pleasure Principle*, can be generalised to "every living creature and is striving to bring it to ruin and to reduce life to its original condition of inanimate matter" (p. 357). When directed outwards towards an object, the death instinct becomes aggressiveness. "The organism preserves its own life, so to say, by destroying an extraneous one" (p. 357). Of course, some of the aggressive instinct, as we have already seen, can be turned inwards, leading to the creation of the conscience. Conscience can also be excessive. In short, the death instinct when directed outwards expends violence that could be turned in on the subject itself. In this way, what we have here is an example of the economic way in which the flow of the death instinct does the work of, even in some ways, *becomes* the instinct for life, a purpose previously reserved for Eros:

> If these forces are turned to destruction in the external world, the organism will be relieved and the effect must be beneficial. This would serve as a biological justification for all the ugly and dangerous impulses against which we are struggling. It must be admitted that they stand nearer to Nature than does our resistance to them for which an explanation needs to be found.
> (Freud, 1985, p. 358)

Now that aggressiveness has been so thoroughly naturalised by Freud, and that the pro-social erotic instinct has been presented as in an un-dis-entanglable relationship with the death drive, it is our own wish for peace that seems curious and unnatural, that befalls us like an accident. Freud concludes, "there is no question of getting rid entirely of human aggressive impulses" (p. 358). The only hope is that they can be diverted, so that they do not lead to war, or that the social instincts that counter-balance war are strengthened. Yet Freud is obviously intrigued by the question: "why do you and I and so many other people rebel so violently against war?" (Freud, 1985, p. 360). In his first attempts to understand war, it was war itself that seemed strange, unfamiliar and needing explanation. So normalised is war now as the context in which human relationships are played out, that it is peace that appears alien and enigmatic. The discussion has come full circle.

There are ample reasons to condemn war for the misery and destruction that it causes. However, Freud believes that there must too be some biological reason why "we" are pacifists (p. 361). The reason is that the "process of civilisation" by which there is "a progressive displacement of instinctual aims and a restriction of instinctual impulses" rests on "organic grounds" (p. 361). War is "in the crassest opposition" to this development of civilisation, and this provokes us to refuse it. This rejection is not merely abstract or intellectual, to Freud, but is in fact "constitutional" (p. 362). Freud's conclusion is to try to dismantle the economic complex he has struggled so hard to theorise. War and civilisation are opposites and "whatever fosters the growth of civilisation works at the same time against war" (p. 362).

If war is the projection of the aggressive instincts outwards, and civilisation depends on the advance of conscience, which can be the direction of aggression inwards, and war is the following of a leader who is a representation of the soldier's ego-ideal, and the object of war is chosen as a result of a tangled process wherein love and aggression cannot be clearly separated, we have a complex economy of ambivalence and the mutual substitution and shared operation of impulses that contest and compete with one another as much as they collaborate. Freud chooses, at different points of his career as a thinker of war, to emphasise one aspect of this complex economy and to suppress or discount others. We have a subject whose relationship to itself combines both an erotic and a death instinct, that may produce itself as the aggressive or excessive operation of conscience; it follows a leader chosen like a love-object as the incarnation of the subject's own ego-ideal, yet because he is a refiguring of the primal father, the leader is also a complex figure, an object of aggression and love, that incites the formation of the conscience precisely because of the irrepressibility of love in the midst of aggression. In turn, the turning of aggression outwards is the result of the irreducible ambivalence of love. Every relationship here is fed by a double orientation that flows backwards between the subject and its objects. Freud at times, strategically, retreats from this complexity in order to find some structure or preference within this complex. This creates inconsistencies, at least of emphasis, throughout Freud's discussions. Indeed, war has seemed to both trigger and complicate his thought in an unsettled pattern of discomfort and anxiety. There is no mistaking the problem that it proposed for psychoanalysis. The inconsistencies and complications here are not to be criticised as flaws in Freud's reasoning, but as evidence of the complexity and instability of the situation he was trying to describe. It is this complexity—and Freud's attempt not to drown in it—that it is important for us to recognise and understand.

In Freud, aggression is an intensification of love, but not a mere continuation or extension of it. Aggression and love form a complex in which they simultaneously incite and ruin one another. Here, we have an account that attempts to analyse in all its difficulty, the problem of the relationship between war and its other that Hobbes' and Kant's accounts revealed but did not confront. It is too simple to see love and aggression or war and its various others as opposite to one another. Freud offers an account in which love is never separable from aggression, and vice versa. War and whatever is seen to stand in opposition to it perpetually entail one another. War constantly pressures our models of orderly civil society, as the very thing that either requires or produces peace. We cannot have peace or order without constant reference to war, and the endless possibility of its re-enactment. War is the meaning of peace, and its double. Freud attempts to psychologise this conundrum, by demonstrating how love and violence always work together in complex processes of investment and identification. The perpetual call for the establishment of an enduring peace is not a solution to the conundrum of war, but a part of it, the insistence on the clash between war and its other that always co-exists with their continuing co-incidence. Yet, history requires a more complex engagement with war not only as a moral problem and a constant human disaster, but as a theoretical aporia, in which tangles, confusions and ambivalences endure unchecked. For all its reductiveness, speculation and treatment of collective problems as if they are always outgrowths of or analogous to individual subjectivity, Freud's account leads us into a set of thinkers who have attempted to deal with war in its thoroughly problematic nature.

Bataille: War, consumption and religion

In Freud, love and aggression are not opposites. Love provokes the aggression it displaces. All human relationships are ambivalent. One way of characterising this ambivalence is to say that to Freud, love and aggression are in an *economic* relationship with one another. In Freudian terms, to describe a relationship as economic means that it is made up of shifting quantities of energy transforming into one another, through rapid and reversible processes of exchange. This trope is developed most thoroughly in the economic model of subjectivity in papers such as "The Unconscious" and "The Economic Problem of Masochism." Here, the dynamics of subjectivity, such as repression, can be understood as the tension between various quantities of energy as they try to contest, overwhelm and absorb one another. Every affect is really made up of different quantities of this one magical substance—energy. This is why they can transmute into one another, and struggle with one another so effectively, because they are all of the same basic nature. Energies shift dramatically. This means that affective states that we would normally describe as opposites should be seen as possible versions of one another. They never lose the state of rivalry or tension with one another, but since they are fundamentally made up of the same stuff, they can easily become one another. An economic relationship, therefore, is one where different states contend with, challenge and struggle with one another, while always being able to become one another. Economic relationships are fundamentally ambivalent therefore, a contradiction within commonality. This complexity is reflected in Freud's understanding of war, in which the enemy is an object of a complex fixation where different types of contradictory emotion are invested, and in which the military organisation is defined by attachment to a leader who is also the focus of intense and contradictory feelings which make the army as a group both effective and also permanently at risk of excess or breakdown.

In the work of Georges Bataille, we see another account of war developed in economic terms. Economics in Bataille is also to be understood in terms of shifting quantities of energy in competition with one another. But, as in Freud, their relationship is a complex one in which apparently contradictory states give rise to one another. Opposite impulses in an economy require one another not because they are dialectical opposites, but because they only arise as apparent contradictions in the form of one another. Bataille's logic is one of tendency and excess, in which contradiction arises through the running-on of an impulse to something necessarily more than itself. Contradiction emerges then within one passage of energy, not through a fundamental contrast of essences. In order to approach Bataille's take on war, it is necessary to understand this complex economics.

To Bataille, economics has traditionally focussed on specific events. These can be as simple as the act of changing a car tyre, or the individual acts of corporations in raising finance. Each of these specific behaviours, according to Bataille, emerges only in and through the general flow of energy in the world. It is possible to act and think as if each of these behaviours is strictly separable from everything else, but this is really a mis-representation of the larger context in which events take place. When we focus on a specific activity, we are blinding ourselves willingly to the complex tangle of relationships in which any event is inevitably situated. To Bataille, human activity is not a set of discontinuous and isolated acts, but the visible segment of a larger process in which human activity "pursues the useless and infinite fulfilment of the universe" (Bataille, 1991, p. 21). In other words, a specific thing is always a mere moment in the dynamic transition of energy from one ephemeral form to another. We choose to focus on the specific and objective, freezing the moment in order to represent the world to ourselves as made up of fixities and stable identities. Yet, the energy that we want to see as frozen into a form is merely in transit towards becoming something else. Ultimately, this larger "something else" is the general expansiveness of energy as the final and inevitable tendency of the universe.

For Bataille, the earth is a site of the play of energy. Energy fulfils certain functions in the world, allowing specific organisms to grow, for example, but it continues to arise (from the sun) in excess of the requirements of simple living things:

> The living organism, in a situation determined by the play of energy on the surface of the globe, ordinarily receives more energy than is necessary for maintaining life: the excess energy (wealth) can be used for the growth of a system (e.g., an organism); if the system can no longer grow, or if the excess cannot be completely absorbed in its growth, it must necessarily be lost without profit; it must be spent, willingly or not, gloriously or catastrophically.
> (Bataille, 1991, p. 21)

As we are accustomed to analysing behaviour and events in the human world in terms of specific operations with identified and recognisable goals, we cannot see this "general" economic logic as the context and mechanism through which specific events become possible. Nor do we see that the key economic problem for societies is what to do with the excess that always over-runs or out-paces the most logical and productive economic processes. This excess is wealth, according to Bataille, and economics must help us understand what will happen to it, how, in short, it will be "squandered," how it will be dissipated in the "useless consumption" (Bataille, 1991, p. 23) that can be its only destiny.

It is necessary, according to Bataille, to overcome our shyness about economics, and to understand these processes of dissipation and use them so that they do not destroy us. Some societies have chosen to use up this excess in the extravagance of rite and festival. In a consumer society, like post-modern capitalism, wealth and waste may be squandered through luxury and pleasure. Yet, if we do not understand and manage this process, we may find ourselves engulfed in war, which emerges as an important and historically irresistible, even necessary form of spending. The existence of an excess of energy that cannot be used up in either festival or petty diversion "has perpetually doomed multitudes of human beings and great quantities of useful goods to the destruction of wars" (Bataille, 1991, p. 24). In Bataille's account, during the long peace from 1815 to 1914, European economies fed their excess back into the growth of productive forces. But this type of expenditure could not be maintained. The production of excess required radical spending, and wars on a grand scale became not the only possible, but at least a likely outcome. Indeed, the particular concentration of excess energy in the expansion of productivity through the nineteenth century determined that the wars that did break out would be of an "extraordinary intensity" (Bataille, 1991, p. 25). The industrial style of warfare that developed through the nineteenth century, then, was not merely a reflection of the nature of modern societies, nor an inevitable consequence of the development of certain technologies. It was a direct result of the capaciousness of Europe's economies. Its intensity was not merely the level of violence that these societies reached because of what they were capable of, and what they determined to do, in an ever-upwardly spiralling competition with one another. It was a necessary result of the amount of wealth that needed to be consumed: excesses of equipment, the result of an endemic and uncontrolled, even unquestioned commitment to the expansion of production beyond any sense of utility. Caught up in this economy loaded with unexpended excess was the human population as well, what Bataille calls "the fleshly aspect of the bony proliferation of the factories" (Bataille, 1991, p. 24). When the economy reached the point of squandering its vast reserves of energy, these other quantities, human bodies, would also be wasted.

For Bataille, then, war, like life itself, is not defined by scarcity. Human groups do not compete with one another for resources. War is not fundamentally teleological or pragmatic. It is not a means to a rational end. Life itself leads inevitably to an outpouring of energy. Parsimony leads necessarily to orgy, not to justified wealth. Wealth itself is not to be seen as social advantage nor material ascendancy, but the simple capacity for squandering. In this, it is neither a moral nor a political category. Wealth is neither privilege nor even power. It is not a category of social identity at all. It is the consequence of the logic of life itself, which runs inevitably on to the accumulation of forces which will need to be expended as luxury. Bataille writes, "The history of life on earth is mainly the effect of a wild exuberance; the dominant event is the development of luxury, the production of increasingly burdensome forms of life" (p. 33). It is in eating, death and sexual reproduction that this superabundance is squandered.

This logic is one we routinely ignore. We prefer to think of ourselves as the productive, husbanding, hoarding animal, preserving stores for an imagined and inevitable future. And this is indeed the first stage of our development:

> The fact is that the revivals of development that are due to human activity, that are made possible or maintained by new techniques, always have a double effect: Initially, they use a portion of the surplus

energy, but then they produce a larger and larger surplus. This surplus eventually contributes to making growth more difficult, for growth no longer suffices to use it up. At a certain point, the advantage of extension is neutralised by the contrary advantage, that of luxury; the former remains operative, but in a disappointing—uncertain, often powerless—way. The drop in the demographic curves is perhaps the first indicator of the change of sign that has occurred: Henceforth what matters *primarily* is no longer to develop the productive forces but to spend their products sumptuously.

At this point, immense squanderings are about to take place (Bataille, 1991, p. 37). The two world wars represented for Bataille not only the most historically insistent, but also the most dramatic example of such squandering: they "organised the greatest orgies of wealth—and of human beings—that history has recorded" (p. 37). In them was exhibited the will to excess and waste for which the human, of all species, is most suited. Bataille writes, "man is the most suited of all living beings to consume intensely, sumptuously, the excess energy offered up by the pressure of life to conflagrations befitting the solar energies of its movement" (p. 37). War is, in fact, the foremost and most telling site where the problem of economics is proposed (p. 40).

How can we make sense of this relationship between war and human reality without succumbing to the seductions of a vitalism that simply overlooks the cruelty and viciousness of historical death? Bataille offers some notional warnings about our need to manage the destructiveness of excess if we do not want to become engulfed by the annihilating flood of energy pouring over us towards exhaustion in an unlimited universe. Yet, he remains fascinated by the inevitable boiling over of energy, and its role in relieving the tension and discipline of a parsimonious social life. The priority given to productivity in post-Reformation European culture prefers the purposeful and objective pattern of achievable goals and measurable outcomes. Energy makes this productivity possible. Since there is only one type of energy, its use for productivity is not alien or counter to the flow of energy in the general economy. It is merely a segment of it. The energy that flows from the sun (Bataille, 1991, p. 28) drives in its end without end towards an unknowable exhaustion. Yet on its path it folds back on itself to form limited and purposeful arrangements. These arrangements—that Bataille calls *restricted* economies—have been the subject of economic thinking as we have known it since Smith. Restricted economies seem at first to be pragmatic, logical and moral. They are sites of planning, meaning and judgement. At first, they would seem to protect us from violence, but there is nothing about them to assure this. The *general* economy defies this steady organisation and calculation, yet the relationship between the two denominations of economy is not one of simple contradiction or opposition. The energy that feeds and allows the restricted economy is merely hesitating, detouring in its still inevitable flow towards extinction and ruin. The energy of the restricted economy, therefore, is the energy of the general economy in its passage towards excess and exhaustion, but merely delayed or momentarily captured by some announced purpose. Indeed, in Bataille's logic, which sees the intensification of investment as inevitably compounding the scale of discharge, the more rich and focussed the injection of energy in any restricted economy, the more likely is the explosion and ebullition that will result when limits crack and logic fails. In other words, the restricted economy is itself in service to the general economy's drift towards violence, even if it is understood and presented in opposite terms.

There is no simple opposition between the restricted and general economies, therefore, and no simple way of preferring one to the other. In any arrangement, we see a restricted economy privileging order, purpose and the result, but this is merely a preliminary stage in the unfolding of energy that must follow in the general economy. Similarly, the general economy cannot be known except through the arrangements of isolation, denotation and identity that belong to the classical logic of the restricted economy. These twin economies are never resolutely separable from one another. The restricted economy offers us practice, order and achievement, but only in the passage towards undoing and redoing that is inevitable in the flow of energy in the general economy. The general economy offers us freedom, but a freedom that we can never fully and completely receive as our living present, that can only be experienced as the momentary or hypothetical undoing of each restricted economy, an undoing made available by the inevitability of generality.

The violence of war is thus not the alternative or refusal of the sensible logic of the restricted economy. It is deeply invested in the structure and operation of each restricted economy, even as the latter denies it. The most logical and pragmatic social arrangement, the most ordered and morally defensible practice pulses with violence in its very bloodlines, therefore, and releases it, not as the defeat or transcendence of logic and order, but as their inevitable consequence. Violence leads out of each restricted economy as the result of the logic by which that economy has been formed. Yet, this also means that violence in turn will be captured and processed by further restriction. We do not and will not know the end of energy. We cannot outlive it, because it can and will always exceed us. The drive of energy to exhaustion and ruin will always be postponed by the continuing formation of newer restricted economies. Yet, the more these restricted economies delay the outburst of energy in the general economy, the more intense they make it. Bataille's discourse then provides us with an image of how formation itself takes place, and the complex logic by which things happen. Identities, entities and programmes form as they unform, and re-form as they pursue the ends of dissipation and they always contain within themselves the simultaneity of both meaning and meaninglessness, mutually producing one another. Let us see how this operates in Bataille's most famous example, one highly relevant to war—the sacrificial rites of the Aztecs.

According to Bataille's account, the Mexicans connected their religious practices to the life of the Sun. Sacrifice was required in order to give the Sun something to eat. In turn, war aimed to garner captives to sacrifice. In this way, the logic of war was not one of conquest, or imperial expansion, but of consumption (Bataille, 1991, p. 49). Bataille identifies war as being of critical significance in such a culture. Children were born to be warriors, as warfare served the most important themes of Aztec religion. Even death on the battlefield was interpreted as a substitute for sacrifice. The warrior killed on the field of battle fed the Sun just as meaningfully as those captives reserved for an elaborate calendar of sacrificial ritual. Yet this warrior society needs, for Bataille, to be distinguished from a military society. He writes,

> The value of war in Aztec society cannot mislead us: It was not a *military* society. Religion remained the obvious key to its workings. If the Aztecs must be situated, they belong among the warrior societies, in which pure, uncalculated violence and the ostentatious forms of combat held sway. The reasoned organisation of war and conquest was unknown to them. A truly *military* society is a venture society, for which war means a development of power, an orderly progression of empire. It is a relatively mild society; it makes a custom of the rational principles of enterprise, whose purpose is given in the future, and it excludes the madness of sacrifice. There is nothing more contrary to military organisation than those squanderings of wealth represented by hecatombs of slaves.
>
> (Bataille, 1991, p. 55)

A military society, according to this account, is a disciplined and purposeful one, governed by a logic of rule and control that reaches out to capture subject lands and peoples. Yet it remains fundamentally logical and mild. Its warfare is a tool or weapon, not a rite. The aim of Aztec warfare is to facilitate a rite. This rite sanctifies the war, which becomes part of religious practice.

Bataille's *Theory of Religion* develops this idea of the relationship between warfare and religion. Bataille starts his account of religion here by looking at the contrast between the human and the animal. The animal is in an unmediated relation with the world: "every animal is *in the world like water in water*," he writes (Bataille, 1989, p. 19). It is not given to animals to objectify what is other to them. Animals do not experience what they are not as objects. This even applies to the things that they eat. This world is inaccessible to a humanity that always protects itself from the world by way of its own sense of meaning, or by commitment to a radical meaninglessness. Both of these descend from the human faith in its ability to assess and know the world. The idea of a world unmediated by the question of meaning—a world without or before world—is unacknowledgable to human consciousness. By identifying objects, starting with the tool, human beings immerse themselves in the world of the continuity and immanence of the animal, while denying it, finding ways to interrupt their relationship with it. Things still remain continuous with the world even though human beings insist they have been separated by being reduced to equipment. "Thus having determined stable and simple things which it is possible to make, men situated on the same plane where the things appeared... elements that were and nonetheless remained continuous with the world, such as animals, plants, other men, and finally, the subject determining itself" (Bataille, 1989, pp. 30-1). Things and even humans themselves have become objectified, artificially and ephemerally, while never actually relinquishing their true continuity with the world: "In the end, we perceive each appearance—subject (ourselves), animal, mind, world—from within and from without at the same time, both as continuity, with respect to ourselves and as object" (p. 31). Although separated, the object shares attributes with the human, and we never fully lose the sense that it may be animate (p. 33).

The human then feels, on the one hand, continuous with the world of immanence, and, on the other hand, that this immanence is being constantly interrupted. Separation and objectification become the norm as the most practical way of dealing with the world, but continuity still beckons as the sacred, to which humans look with a kind of fascination, but also impotent horror (Bataille, 1989, p. 36). This complexity encourages a sense that there is an opposition between the world of the sacred and the profane. "The reality of a profane world, of a world of things and bodies, is established opposite a holy and mythical world" (Bataille, 1989, p. 37). Human reality spans the divide between the sacred and the profane, sometimes falling back into the world of the real to which objects belong, and sometimes struck by the divine: "Insofar as it is spirit, the human reality is holy, but it is profane in so far as it is real. Animals, plants, tools and other controllable things form a real world with the bodies that control them, a world subject to and traversed by divine forces, but fallen" (p. 38).

The human controls and suppresses the real in order to demonstrate his separation from it. The eating of meat, for example, is the human way of signalling our own non-objectivity. The killing, cooking and eating of living stuff attests that it is what the human is not (p. 39). This validation of the human comes at the price of a separation from the natural world which must now be objectified, and consequently there is a loss of immanence. "Nature becomes man's property but it ceases to be immanent to him. It is his on the condition that it is closed to him" (p. 41). The human then experiences a double alienation. Humans aim to confirm the objectivity of nature in order to assert their divinity, but, at the same time, this self-identity deriving from the natural world makes humans feel remote from the immanence that could confirm and strengthen the quality of their divinity. When we work with things, we become like them. "All this is foreign to the immanent immensity, where there are neither separation nor limits. In the degree that he is the immanent immensity, that he is being, that he is of the world, man is a stranger for himself" (Bataille, 1989, p. 42).

The centrality of sacrifice to religion is explained by this complex and problematic relationship between the human and objectivity. The aim of sacrifice is to destroy not the sacrificed thing itself, but its objectivity. "The thing—only the thing—is what sacrifice means to destroy in the victim...it draws the victim out of the world of utility and restores it to that of unintelligible caprice" (Bataille, 1989, p. 43). Sacrifice, then, challenges the logic that sees the real world only as the site of the validation of utility and future-thinking: "Sacrifice is the antithesis of production, which is accomplished with a view to the future; it is consumption that is concerned only with the moment...in sacrifice the offering is rescued from all utility" (p. 49).

This annihilation of objectivity involves an inevitable challenge to the daylight logic of consciousness, which is itself a creature of the real: "the return to immanent intimacy implies a beclouded consciousness" (p. 45). This complication of coherent consciousness also means that the world of intimacy undermines the logic of individuality: "intimacy is violence, and it is destruction, because it is not compatible with the positing of the separate individual" (p. 51). The separate individual is squarely on the side of work and objectivity. It "is of the same nature as the thing" (p. 51). This individuality is struck by anguish when it confronts its own alienation from the world of intimacy. Individuality is anguish. Yet because we can only experience the sacred from the point of view of the individuality that orients our daily life, the sacred is always to be experienced as a "trembling of the individual...[as] holy, sacred and suffused with anguish" (p. 52).

The danger of intimacy and consumption is managed, therefore, because these two are only ever experienced as a gap in the coherence of the real world and its concomitant individuality. The festival in which the immersion in intimacy is most intensely organised must have a double edge, therefore, "an aspiration for destruction" and "a conservative prudence that regulates and limits it" (Bataille, 1989, p. 54). The festival must combine the world of intimacy with the real world in the same way that restricted and general economies must imply, engage and produce one another. "The festival is not a true return to immanence but rather an amicable reconciliation, full of anguish, between the incompatible necessities" (p. 55). The combination of mildness and civility, on the one hand, with horror and mutilation, on the other, captures the intense convergence of Bataille's world. In religion, what is at stake is not the logical structure of cosmic identities. A religion of cosmic politics ordered by a personalised authority who legislates morality is a real world schema, a constituted autocracy, knowable and reassuring in its ability to save us from danger. Religion, for Bataille, demands the unseating of such a constituted order of salvation, by immersing us in the intimate drama of destruction and chaos. It takes place not as the elevation and salvation of the individual but in the intensity of the subject's division from itself. The human is the "subject-object" (Bataille, 1989, p. 56) straddling the divide between intimacy and the real. It must be experienced not as a fallen angel seeking its restoration to a transcendental completion as unity. Intimacy is offered as the intensity of a collision between two mutually defying and irreconcilable aspects of humanity, a collision that can never be either logically resolved into contradiction or relieved by a meaningful separation.

> Man is the being that has lost, and even rejected, that which he obscurely is, a vague intimacy. Consciousness could not have become clear in the course of time if it had not turned away from its awkward

contents, but clear consciousness is itself looking for what it has itself lost, and what it must lose again as it draws near to it. Of course what it has lost is not outside it; consciousness turns away from the obscure intimacy of consciousness itself.

(Bataille, 1989, p. 57)

At first sight, war seems to be analogous to sacrifice. The festival turns violence inwards and thus reveals for a society its problematic but necessary relationship with intimacy. War, however, is violence turned outwards, and although it may seem to reveal, as only violence can, the relationship with life, it ends in failure, by confirming the individuality that has been risked:

[War] is a disorderly eruption whose external direction robs the warrior of the intimacy he attains. And if it is true that warfare tends in its own way to dissolve the individual through a negative wagering of the value of his own life, it cannot help but enhance his value in the course of time by making the surviving individual the beneficiary of the wager.

(Bataille, 1989, p. 58)

In festival, the logic of the real is sundered, and the subject is exposed to the intimacy that is its truth and which individuality as a mode of the subject is used to cover up. Warfare opens on intimacy, but it never finally requires that the individual lose itself in the intensity that it thus always fails to deal with. Individuality gains prestige because it seems momentarily to connect with intimacy, though it quickly withdraws into its regular instrumental logic. The strength of the warrior then "is in part a strength to lie" (Bataille, 1989, p. 58). The well-rehearsed patterns of the real are not exploded in military war, but endlessly recovered, and confirmed: "the warrior reduces his fellow-men to servitude. He thus subordinates violence to the most complete reduction of mankind to the order of things" (p. 59). Violence, which in its bottomless darkness had seemed to expose the continuity and ineluctable irretrievability of life for meaning, becomes a tool or device. The momentary open-ness of the warrior to violence is made safe for reality by the reduction of violence to the instrumental. The sacredness of the warrior is faked. "The warrior's nobility is like a prostitute's smile, the truth of which is self-interest" (p. 59).

Sacrifice of the slaves promises to return to the warrior some of the possibility opened by the interior violence of the festival. It means that the profit of the exterior violence of war would be annihilated. Killing captured slaves rather than subjecting them to forced work would be a type of internal violence. The external violence of war profits by capturing usable slaves. To destroy them would be to insist that the destruction of utility means more than the capture of profit or disabling of enemies. This too would mean that the group has not pursued war simply in order to confirm its success in the real, nor the discreteness of its individuality. Yet, since the sacrifice involved is of the captured, of the profits of war and not of things central to the society, not of the social fabric itself, the sacrifice which is the only possible glory in war is relatively cheapened. Consumption is dangerous, shocking and extreme. In the end, royal or sacred victims, whose immolation would have represented the society's most authentic preparedness for confronting intimacy, are substituted by captured slaves and proxy victims. Little then is risked. Sacredness is no longer to be fully confronted. "The primacy of consumption could not resist that of military force" (Bataille, 1989, p. 61).

Bataille then extends this contrast between a violence directed inwards and one directed towards the exterior. The military order arises, using violence not as a festival of the meaning that defies meaning similar to sacrifice, but instead, it turns violence into a means of imperial expansion. The military order then is anathema to the will-to-intimacy associated with religious consumption. The military order refuses sacrifice and abhors violence turned within:

> The military order is contrary to the forms of spectacular violence that correspond more to the unbridled explosion of fury than to the rational calculation of effectiveness. It no longer aims at the greatest expenditure of forces, as an archaic social system did in warfare and festivals. The expenditure of forces continues, but it is subjected to a principle of maximum yield: if the forces are spent, it is with a view to the acquisition of greater forces. Archaic society confined itself in warfare to the rounding up of slaves. In keeping with its principles, it could compensate for these acquisitions by means of ritual slaughters. The military order organizes the yield of wars into slaves, that of slaves into labour. It makes conquest a methodical operation, for the growth of an empire.
>
> (Bataille, 1989, p. 66)

The culture of empire is no longer that of an individual community. It is an order of things which defines and controls the real, using a logic of universality. The military order then corresponds to the development of a particular philosophy. As the military order pursues the logic of integrating the objectified things of the world into its own order of things, the role of consciousness is an equally universal and totalising contemplation, a "measured reflection of the world of things" (Bataille, 1989, p. 69). Religion becomes trapped in the profane order, seeking legislative norms and identities rather than the vital encounter in the moment with the intensity of intimacy, norms which "rationalise and moralise divinity, in the very movement where morality and reason are divinised" (p. 71). Dualism becomes the governing structure of all valuation, to which the human becomes subordinate. "At the level of the dualistic conception, no vestige of the ancient festivals can prevent reflective man, whom reflection constitutes, from being, at the moment of his fulfilment, man of lost intimacy" (p. 74). In this world, mind and the good are associated with one another and so too are evil and matter. "A world is defined in which free violence has only a negative place" (p. 77).

Yet, humanity does not simply evolve its institutions and practices beyond the logic of intimacy. The military order may only "[aim] to give the order of things, as it is, a universal form and value" (p. 90), but the problem of violence remains unsolved. The military order initiates a kind of cultural logic that attempts to close off and seal over the fertility and drama of the intimate, by reinforcing the status of the real, of the object, of the profane, of consciousness and of the disciplined straitening of "the individual" in all its manifestations, social, metaphysical and moral. Yet, this order is no less conditioned by violence than the culture of intimacy it is attempting to suppress. In fact, the whole order of the profane that the military order attempts to pioneer and protect must continue to extend intimacy's reach negatively. The god that is the culmination of this development embodies this instability. Bataille writes,

> The god is an exclusion of violence and there can be no breaking of the order of separate things, no intimacy, without violence; the god of goodness is limited by right to the violence with which he excludes violence, and he is divine, open to intimacy, only in so far as he preserves the old violence within him, which he does not have the rigor to exclude, and to this extent he is not the god of reason, which is the truth of goodness. In theory this involves a weakening of the moral divine in favour of evil.
>
> (Bataille, 1989, pp. 80–1)

The most virgin God is still the result of an exposure to the intimacy of violence.

What then is the economy of war? Violence in itself opens the possibility of human access to the intimacy of continuity from which we feel detached in our real-world domain of practicality, objectivity and individuality. There are broadly speaking two modes of warfare: that in service to sacrifice and that of the military order. The warfare of sacrifice opens warrior-violence to the greater violence of intimacy. The warrior's fighting aims to procure slaves who become the wealth of a society, which the society then sacrifices in order to direct violence against the inhibiting internal structure of the real and the restricted economy. The society turns violence within in order to escape into the domain of the intimate. On the other hand, the military order also organises violence, but it uses the slaves it captures as labourers in service of the expansion and confirmation of the economic logic of the real and the object.

The violence of the military order, however, is impossible without reference to the larger violence of intimacy. The violence it organises and disciplines can never be absolutely distinguished from the violence that carries on into the intensity and risk of generality. The violence that ends in conquest, empire, and the practical logic of dominance and exploitation opens on intimacy, uses its chaotic energy, but then withdraws in order to conform to the rigour of system and purpose. It follows the trajectory of the violence whose aim is to lose itself in intimacy. It needs this violence and respects its intensity, but spurns it, even, in the end, mocking it, ruling it out of order. The religious violence of the warrior is romanticised by the military order, but is finally unavailable to it, because it would risk the discipline and purposefulness that rationalises its social role. The military order and the trajectory of the warrior are in the same relationship with one another as the restricted and general economies. The restricted economy can only develop as a circumscribed part of the larger passage of energy towards expansion, excess, and finally exhaustion. It draws on this flow of energy, but must in the end, loudly repudiate it. The military order follows the trajectory of warrior-violence towards an intimacy that orients it, but that it must ultimately reject and abominate.

We have seen in Freud, how the structure of the military group both incited and constrained violence, encouraging its drive towards cruelty and annihilation, while demanding its directedness and discipline. The consequence is that psychologically the soldier lives beyond his means, always prey to the drive to excessive violence cultivated within him, but that is insistently identified as illegal. In Bataille, the purposeful violence of the soldier always risks rolling on into the excessiveness of intimacy, in which all meanings and values will be extinguished, because its impetus has always been to be open on such violence. Discipline must be ruthless because atrocity beckons, and is far from foreign to the military. There would be no military order without the intimacy which the military order must resist and repudiate. In short, the violence of the military order will always be a version of the religious violence of the warrior, and will always adopt, if only momentarily, some of its features and temptations. At times, in its commemorations of its dead and its martial ceremonies, it will even ape, albeit in a vanilla way, aspects of the festival of intimacy. Yet, following the logic of economy, it will always deny, constrain and conceal this connection. It is in this relationship that the apparently irresistible attractiveness of warfare as entertainment remains live. There is no military order, no matter how disciplined, that does not at some point connect with the intensity, display and charisma of radical intimacy.

In economic accounts of warfare, therefore, the principle of military order attempts to connect war with the ordinary world of social order and progress. Yet, because it is reliant on violence, it must always remain open on those impulses that destroy sociality, which Bataille connects with the religious drive to intimacy, and the general flow of energy in the universe. The violence that risks but denies violence is an instantiation of the doubleness of Bataille's economics. The military order is a counter-violent violence. It operates what it refuses, it denies what it wants. Its violence conforms to a logic of reason, purpose and identity, all of which consider themselves the enemies of chaos, intimacy and continuity, but they can only be played out by way of the violence that keeps these opposites in contact with one another. The violence military violence abhors never lets it go. Military violence never becomes another violence. Not only is military violence conditioned by the violence of the intimate order, since it is always designed as a way of dealing with it, but it also poaches from it. It is the violence of the intimate order in denial of itself, in the same way that the restricted economy operates the energy of the general economy that it refuses to know.

We will see in the next section, on Deleuze and Guattari's "war-machine," another account of the necessary but contradictory relationship within the organisation of official violence, between the military as it is co-ordinated with society, on the one hand, and the intimacy of the warrior-cult, on the other. Before we do this, however, it is worth making a series of observations about the consequences of Bataille's thinking of war for our study of the complex relationship between war and its other.

The military order, as we have seen, occupies the liminal space between the logic and order of imperium, and the chaos of the warrior. It must both enact and repudiate the warrior impulse. We have seen how Bataille identifies how it fails to commit to the complete enactment of warrior-dom. Yet, it connects enough with intimacy to cause intimacy to redefine the social. Transgression in Bataille is the process by which the radical chaos of the general economy is incorporated into the logic of civil society (see Bataille, 1986, pp. 29–146). In this way, it both enacts generality and controls it, restoring the dominance of logical order. Transgression expresses a society's engagement with the irrational and excessive flows of energy that have made all its systems and logics possible, but which also exceed and threaten them. Engagement with these flows is a fulfilment of our nature, but it must be felt as a contradiction of our normal, rational, life, which it simultaneously confirms. War is an example of transgression. It opens up possibilities of ecstasy, intensity and violence, while retrospectively constructing before and to endure beside and beyond them, an imagined culture of reason, innocence and meaning. Dissociation and excess require this zone as the antecedent of transgression, in fact, what is to be transgressed. Reason, morality and purpose then are constructed as the necessary counterpart and context of excessive violence and disarray. Following this logic, war then cannot be simply something executed by "the social" nor can it be a simple version of it. It defines the social as the locus of an innocence that violence is to transgress, a rightness that needs to be defied by a brutality that confirms and consolidates it. Innocence thus needs war as that which both confirms and justifies it as innocence.

Secondly, this process of transgression requires a rethinking of subjectivity. The subjectivity of normal social life is an artificial construct made available by the flows of energy, but perched precariously upon them. Such specific, individual or localised subjectivities are mere fictions, chimera even. Bataille was not afraid to say that the truth of subjectivity was available, but only through the process of transgression. Only the subject that could instantiate the flows of the cosmic energy field was authentic to Bataille, and humans recognised and tried to live this subjectivity. The figure that incarnated or represented this asymptotic subject, Bataille called the sovereign. The sovereign embodied a subjectivity that lived the intense basic truth of cosmic force. Individual identity was only ever a pathetic degradation of this heroic possibility. The subject of war, then, is radical intimacy imagined as livable, and is in defiance of any of the constraints and order that define conventional subjectivity. This sovereignty is both the same as and different to the one Agamben derives from Benjamin and Carl Schmitt. It is a logic of exception from historical accountability. However, in Bataille crucially, it is less a hardened singular authority than a dream of the instantiation of radical chaos, one that subjectivity aims to emulate in its truth. As Derrida argues in "Force of Law" and most recently in *Rogues*, this sovereignty must be seen in its dangerous doubleness, as both the risk of the worst and the only promise of justice.

Thirdly, Bataille thought that rituals of sacrifice proposed a question. Rituals dramatised the human need to make contact with the forces of the cosmos, but why did they have to take this form: the slaughter of a human being? What was specific about this process that made it sensible as an engagement with cosmic truth? As we have seen he emphasised the fact that sacrifice annihilated its object. It took something we might recognise as a version of ourselves, another human subject more or less equivalent to us, and it turned this subject into an object and then destroyed it. Bataille argued that this process of annihilation of the object defined what consumption was all about. It was simply the human act of denial of our own objectivity. By thoroughly destroying the object, human beings separated themselves from the possibility of considering themselves to be objects, and thus showed that they could not be reduced to the level of the merely calculable that defined the rational practices of their daily lives. The human approach to objects in general involves, first, this insistence on their reduction to pure objectivity, and secondly, on their being used up, being annihilated as a show of control over and contempt for the objects that we believe we are showing are ontologically different from us. War then turns what is not an object into an object, and then annihilates it in order to show that we are not like it. It does this by first annihilating any impression or trace of alternative subjectivity in the object, and then consuming it as an object, by physically destroying it in order to show the triumph of its own claim to not only exclusive subjectivity, but a subjectivity projected backwards to us from the radical intimacy in which our truth resides.

It would be possible to use this insight to speculate in subjective-cultural terms on the US government's response to the terrorist attacks of September 11, 2001. Horrified at being objectified, being turned into a passive target by Al-Qaida, the United States mounted a massive attempt to reclaim the prerogatives of subjectivity. It needed to turn itself from object to subject, by insisting on the objectivity of others, at first in Afghanistan and then Iraq. These others must have their subjectivity minimised—in the case of Iraq, by the ontology of the nation being reduced from millions of people to one demonised name ("Saddam

Hussein"), by the obscuring of the casualty rates of the Iraqi people, and by having their political aspirations reduced to being identical with the middle of any Western democracy. This objectification of subjectivity licenses violence and restores subjectivity to the United States. More than vengeance, more than strategy or oil, the original political popularity of the Iraq venture could be seen as an attempt to reclaim a subjectivity lost by the mystery and abject confusion of having been objectified.

In sum, then, war allows us access to a triumphal and intimate subjectivity we feel is our truth, by annihilating the other first as subject and then as object. Although this project fulfils us, we always represent and understand it as a transgression, a contradiction of our normal rational innocence. This latter point helps us to answer the question of how a warlike culture with a history of relentless conquest and genocide is able to believe itself so peace-loving and innocent. The logic of war is understood as an adventure beyond innocence and reason and its conventional liberal interiorities into an intimacy that provides a subjectivity beyond constraint. An innocent domain then is perpetually retrospectively reinvented by the wars it requires as the thing that war leaves behind. Similarly, defining a social rift, or even a policy, as a war—war on crime, war on drugs, culture wars—retrospectively identifies the social as a transgressed innocence, a site of authentic self-identity and normality threatened by drugs, the poor, liberal dissent, obesity and so on.

According to Bataille's double logic, then, war unfolds as a transgression of radical innocence and of reason. Innocence and war would be part of one complex, necessary to one another, but they would be understood to be and represented as fundamentally separate, and notionally opposite to one another. How does this complex relationship play itself out? Besides its transgressive nature, we have identified two other things about war: its understanding of subjectivity as radical intimacy and its will to annihilation of its object. It achieves this latter by first erasing any trace of subjectivity in the object, and then destroying it as object. The aim here, according to Bataille's theory of consumption, is to arrogate subjectivity to oneself, by rendering any notion of the subjectivity and consequently the being of the other impossible. One's own subjectivity emerges only as an *über*-subjectivity, as the supersession of subjectivity in an act of destruction. The destruction of the subjectivity of the war-object also then involves the destruction or at least the surpassing of the warrior's own subjectivity. In destroying the subjectivity of the other, it imagines itself out in the stream of larger entropic energy that Bataille saw as the meaning of the cosmos. The logic of the annihilation of the other and the intimacy of subjectivity are the same logic therefore.

The war/other complex can be seen then as the self-overcoming of the subject by pursuing the will-to-annihilation of the object. This defines the society that goes to war in its radical disloyalty to itself. The society-at-war produces this logic in its both peaceful and aggressive phases: in military force, police tactic, media campaign or social policy, but also in its economics, its consumption and its consumerism, yet the society-at-war is able to insist on the radical disjunction between its different phases, a disjunction it cannot even really produce let alone stabilise. (Where exactly would the dividing line fall?) This common ground, even when disguised by a resort to logic of transgression, indicates the dominant mode of the globalising West, on its mission as the ultra-violent bestower, even incarnation, of peace.

By constructing its own subjectivity as the supersession of subjectivity through the annihilation of all alternative subjectivities, the subjectivity of the society-at-war is at work in war, but not at stake. Not only does war provide an image of innocence by representing its violent self as other to society, but the self-overcoming subject never has content enough to be in any way answerable. Because its logic requires the annihilation of its object, it can refuse to acknowledge the position from which it could be interrogated or accused. Hence the refusal of the United States to imagine being answerable to the International Criminal Court. The warfare society is protected from accusation, *until it is defeated*, and becomes an object again. The West will not suffer interrogation of its innocence while it remains triumphant. However, what is at stake is not mere self-delusion, but the logic by which war can emerge in the unfolding of a social project that can maintain its self-image of peace and innocence. This is not done by willing blindness, but *because war is available only by way of a complex that installs innocence with, and even as, it.*

War, then, is double. Bataille's economics is truly an anti-metaphysics: it provides an account of the fundamental logic of the universe, while, at the same time, locating the coherence of accounts and the self-identity of logic as part of the artificiality that the larger context defies. This is not a theoretical failing so much as indicative of the problematic nature of any identity under this dispensation. The situation with war is no different. The military order draws on the violence that threatens to ruin society in order to enlarge the social. The risks this involves are immense. War becomes necessary to the social, while installing what the daylight logic of the social can only see as insanity at its very heart. We will soon see a more stark version of this relationship in our analysis of Deleuze and Guattari. Bataille's account articulates how war and its other can develop in a problematic double relationship, one in which the two are inextricably linked, while remaining a threat to one another. This goes some of the way towards solving the problem that encumbered the arguments of Hobbes and Kant, whose attempts to see war and its other as opposed to one another were challenged by the fact that, in their accounts, the two were fundamentally inalienable. The challenge is to see if the complexity of Bataille's argument demands that we adhere to the idiosyncrasy of his anti-metaphysics. It is to Derrida that we will soon turn to see if this is possible – first, however, a development of Bataille's understanding of the complex relationship between the military order and civil society in Deleuze and Guattari's theory of the war-machine.

Deleuze and Guattari: Owning the war-machine

In an economy, intimacy and the real generate and depend on one another in ever-complicating cycles of mutual sustenance, but there remains an irreducible clash between them, a failure of adequation, a suspicion, a non-endorsement, a will to frustration that must be recognised, a mutual violence even. This clash is always regenerated in the inspiration that is directed towards making them one. The relationship cannot work without this necessary mutual dis-satisfaction. Opposition without separation, contradiction without resolution, difference in indifference, the economy is defined by the transmutation of like into like un-like. Deleuze and Guattari's theory of nomadology and the war-machine emphasises the contrast in collaboration that resides at the heart of economic thinking. In this way, it insists on the most fundamental achievement of those who think of war as an economy: it allows the irreducible contradiction between war and its other to be sustained through their co-operation. It provides a language in which this complex can be co-ordinated. War is available to society, but only by way of an irreducible threat, not only to its order, but to its culture as well. Deleuze and Guattari present this contrast as fundamental to art and technology as much as it is to politics and sovereignty.

Deleuze and Guattari's argument begins by drawing on Georges Dumézil's account of the double figure-head of the State. Political authority conventionally relies on a difficult but always potentially systematic relationship between magician-king and jurist-priest (Deleuze and Guattari, 1987, p. 351). What is omitted from this double-headed monster is war. The State either resorts to non-warrior forms of violence such as the police and jailers or it organises a bureaucratic military-function that subordinates war and warriors to its own logic.

Like the warrior in Bataille, who remains unassimilated to the military order, what Deleuze and Guattari call the war-machine is in itself alien to the State, and fundamentally antipathetic to it. It is the bearer of an altogether different culture, one that the State will always find foreign, obscure, unstable and challenging:

> As for the war machine in itself, it seems to be irreducible to the State apparatus, to be outside its sovereignty and prior to its law: it comes from elsewhere. *Indra, the warrior god, is in opposition to Varuna no less than to Mitra.* He can no more be reduced to one or the other than he can constitute a third of their kind. Rather, he is like a pure and immeasurable multiplicity, the pack, an irruption of the ephemeral and the power of metamorphosis.
> (Deleuze and Guattari, 1987, p. 352)

The war-machine then is something "in itself," something that even when it is used and controlled by the State remains fundamentally alien to it. Similarly, the war machine is not a rival to the two heads of the State, instead providing a third alternative.

> He unties the bond just as he betrays the pact. He brings a furor to bear against sovereignty, a celerity against gravity, secrecy against the public, a power against sovereignty, a machine against the apparatus. He bears witness to another kind of justice, one of incomprehensible cruelty at times, but at others of unequalled pity as well (because he unties bonds...).
> (Deleuze and Guattari, 1987, p. 352)

There is only an ephemeral order in the culture of the war-machine, one that privileges spontaneity, energy, excess, caprice, obscurantism and shattering, violence but not order. The logic of identity and unity is itself foreign to the war-machine, which is the principle of irreducible plurality and instability. The war-machine, in Deleuze and Guattari, represents a secularised instantiation of what Bataille calls intimacy. It incarnates change and plurality, the undefinable mystery of transformation. "[The warrior-nomad] bears witness, above all, to other relations with women, with animals, because he sees all things in relations of becoming, rather than implementing binary distinctions between 'states': a veritable becoming-animal of the warrior, a becoming-woman, which lies outside dualities of terms as well as correspondences between relations" (Deleuze and Guattari, 1987, p. 352).

The magician-king and jurist-priest may be figures of an esoteric order, but they require and reproduce a culture committed to the endurance of sovereignty and practical achievement. They promise continuity and calm, even one interrupted by the momentary spasm of the festival or the palace coup. They promise the steady elaboration of meaning through continuous time, in the form of historical narrative, institutional identity and deliberative justice. The war-machine abominates all these things, resisting them at every level, seeking no revelation of hidden truth through historical progress, perhaps not thinking of the future at all, in fact. The war-machine delivers a becoming-other that will never make sense of a justice more complex than spontaneous anger or sentimental pity.

To the State-thinking that organises us and our discourse, the man of war is a fool, a failure, an eccentricity, a dead-end, a by-product of a history that had more enduring and more valuable prizes to offer. He cannot be recognised by the State as something meaningful or purposeful. He is a joke, a madman or a usurper (Deleuze and Guattari, 1987, p. 354). This is because of the limitations of State-logic, according to Deleuze and Guattari: the war-machine defies the logic of structured, conceptual thought. The State relies on a thinking of interiority, of structured and consistent ontology, of the city, where the warrior is a creature of the outside, of the plains. Nomadism is "a pure form of exteriority" (p. 354). A problem arises in that conceptual thought is part of the culture of the State, and is thus unable to recognise nomadism except by conflating it with one or other of the poles of the State apparatus. Since we cannot think the war-machine, the easiest thing for us to do is to refigure it in terms of something we can not only think, but that is the legitimation of conceptual thinking itself: the State. The war-machine can then appear sometimes as "the magic violence of the State, at other times [as] the State's military institution" (Deleuze and Guattari, 1987, p. 354). This disguises the fundamental foreign-ness at the heart of the State/war-machine relation: "The State has no war machine of its own: it can only appropriate one in the form of a military institution, one that will continually cause it problems" (p. 355). The warrior himself seems superfluous, doomed and self-destructive, even though he can be of use to the State. He has lost from the start. All he can hope for is an unstable relationship with the State, in which it subordinates the warrior's ways to its own bureaucratic organisation.

In Bataille, the military order insisted on the discipline of individuality and the purposefulness of strategy as a counter to the impulse towards intimacy. It was the warrior who was most in touch with intimacy, and when he was incorporated into the military order, he brought with him the trace of intimacy, and all its dangers: chaos, pointlessness and the risk of atrocity. The will to puncture the sealed world of work and the real and gain access to the flow of continuity and intimacy required a violence that was directed inwards, a kind of self-mutilation that manifested scorn for husbandry, logic and purpose. This inwardly directed violence exceeded the hard logic of the individuality that incarnated the ethos of self-discipline and work. The military order recognised this impulse, but negatively. Instead of encouraging the deconstruction of individuality in the violent quest for intimacy, it resisted it, confirming individuality not just at the level of the subjective monad, but at the level of the community, the tribe, or the group, each of which individualised and homogenised themselves by directing violence outwards. The function of the military order then was to exploit the longing for intimacy by making its violence practical.

In Bataille, the domain in which to understand the meaning of warfare, prior to its appropriation by the military order, is not first and foremost politics, sociology or psychology. It is not gender, nor ethnicity nor biology, but *religion*. Thus, pure warfare in Bataille must be understood not as a simple pragmatic device, a mechanism by which things get done, rivals are silenced, sexual partners lured, property seized, ground gained, ascendancy symbolised, vengeance satisfied, dominance assured and so on. It is the fulfilment of the logic of a certain (anti-)metaphysics. War must be understood in itself as something, not as a means to an end. Deleuze and Guattari confirm this when they argue for the specificity of war as something not needed by bureaucratic city states, and as such as an invention of the nomads. They also see warfare as something to be understood in terms of its general cultural logic rather than its specific historical uses.

There are ways in which Deleuze and Guattari's construction of the relationship between warfare and metaphysics can be compared to Bataille's. In Bataille, war evades logic and the real, as we have seen. In Deleuze and Guattari, the man of war is condemned and ridiculed by the State, because the conceptual logic that defines and advances the constitutive ambition of conceptual thought is itself a State-thought, a logic that validates and assures the values of permanency, enduring institutions and predictable systems and values. This thought cannot accommodate the war-machine, which privileges metamorphosis over identity, manifestation over representation, and the unrepeatable event over the constituted institution. Conceptual thinking, because of its own biases, is unable to respect or even recognise the culture of the war-machine.

However, there is at least one significant way in which Deleuze and Guattari seem to part from Bataille and it is over the question of religion. In Deleuze and Guattari's war-machine, the logic of intimacy is discussed as if it is manifest as physical people. The thinking of the war-machine presses on us not in the way the invisible and esoteric may momentarily reveal themselves in the gaps that proliferate in the apparently seamless insistence of daily life. The war-machine fills the margins and unmapped extramural zones of our experience, forcing us to recognise that other ways of thinking and living inhabit our world. It is altogether a different outside to the outside within of intimacy. Yet, how literally are we to take the nomadology of Deleuze and Guattari? How much is it an elaborate philosophical fiction, generated by a methodology that proceeds not positivistically but analogically in order to mark out and confuse the unacknowledged limits of conceptual metaphysical thinking? This would certainly be consistent with the argument of their *What is Philosophy?* (Deleuze and Guattari, 1994). Their essay is then perhaps not about nomads but about the thought haunted by the idea of them, and they exist half way between dim but deep memories of atrocity, on the one hand, and the categorical refusal of the impermanent as a kind of horror, on the other hand, but not in themselves as flesh and blood historical people. The argument says as much: the nomads are outside of even the avant-garde conceptual thinking being practised here. Therefore they cannot exist or be discussed other than as figures at play in, or putting pressure on, a logic that refuses them. In this way, they are very much like the intimate, in that they can be known only in terms of the gaps within the conceptual thinking they defy. Nomads, like intimacy, therefore cannot be said to exist in any conventional meaning of the term. They lack ontology, because every language that could possibly describe them refuses them. They are the roving limit-thought of conceptualism. Thinking of war and its other economically identifies metaphysics as occupying a particular position in the complex. The complex then has to be thought outside of or beyond metaphysics. As we will see with our discussion of Derrida below, it leads inevitably towards deconstruction.

The war-machine then is less to be taken as a representation of the separate culture of real people, so much as the interior limit of State thinking. Deleuze and Guattari allow Bataille's economic thinking about war and its concomitant problematisation of a conceptual and rational metaphysics to be secularised, yet it endures more as the difficulty and instability of the relationship between identity and provisionality, and between stability and volatility, than it does as a representation of a distinctive historical culture. The relationship between the State and the war-machine must be seen as economic rather than dialectical. It is the way in which excess, danger and plurality are inscribed within even the most rigorous thinking of identity, and are always available to it, as the necessary limit or problem of its imperium and the means of its renewal, even when they seem most to threaten it. As in Bataille, the thought of radical chaos is in an inextricable relationship with the philosophy of order, even though it is a danger and a foreigner to it.

What then is the exact nature of the relationship between the war-machine and the State apparatus? In a discussion of Kleist, Deleuze and Guattari define the exteriority of the war-machine in terms of its relationship to conventional subjectivity, which is implicitly connected with the logic of the State. In Kleist:

> Feelings become uprooted from the interiority of a "subject," to be projected violently outward into a milieu of pure exteriority that lends them an incredible velocity, a catapulting force: love or hate, they are no longer feelings but affects.
> (Deleuze and Guattari, 1987, p. 356)

In contrast to feelings, affects traverse limits and identities. They "transpierce the body like arrows, they are weapons of war" (Deleuze and Guattari, 1987, p. 356). This reinvents time in terms of "an endless succession of catatonic episodes or fainting spells, and flashes or rushes" (p. 356), defining a subjectivity beyond subjectivity in terms of "a succession of flights of madness and catatonic freezes in which no subjective interiority remains" (p. 356). Deleuze and Guattari then ask,

> Could it be that it is at the moment the war-machine ceases to exist, conquered by the State, that it displays to the utmost its irreducibility, that it scatters into thinking, loving, dying, or creating machines that have at their disposal vital or revolutionary powers capable of challenging the conquering State? Is the war machine already overtaken, condemned, appropriated as part of the same process whereby it takes on new forms, undergoes a metamorphosis, affirms its irreducibility and exteriority, and deploys that milieu of pure exteriority that the occidental man of the State, or the occidental thinker, continually reduces to something other than itself?
> (Deleuze and Guattari, 1987, p. 356)

Here, the war-machine is not simply the outside of the neatly formed State, but that outside which must be *redrawn* by the logic of the State. It must be drawn within and transformed. It is therefore at work in the logic of the State but as something else, something at first glance hostile and antipathetic to itself. Yet this is where it is most irreducibly itself. As it is erased, it is licensed. As it is taken over, it is released. As it is mocked, it is encouraged. As it is forgotten, it is reinstituted as everything but itself.

Traditionally, the State has been seen as a more advanced form than nomadism. Nomadism, and primitive societies in general, did not form States according to conventional thinking, because they did not develop complex-enough economies or political organisations with sufficient internal differences. Deleuze and Guattari, however, quote Clastres' counter-argument that perhaps it was not a failure on the part of "primitive" societies, but their determined resistance that resulted in their evading the State-form. And perhaps, Clastres argues, it was precisely war itself that was the logic whereby they ensured this frustration of the evolution of the State:

> But Clastres goes further, identifying war in primitive societies as the surest mechanism directed against the formation of the State: *war maintains the dispersal and segmentarity of groups, and the warrior himself is caught in the process of accumulating exploits leading him to solitude and a prestigious but powerless death.* Clastres can thus invoke natural Law while reversing its principle proposition: just as Hobbes saw clearly that *the State was against war, so war is against the State* and makes it impossible. It should not be concluded that war is a state of nature, but rather that it is the mode of a social state that wards off and prevents the State.
>
> (Deleuze and Guattari, 1987, p. 357)

The war-machine is organised in a way that resists the formation of centralised power. Gangs often limit the ability of their leaders to adopt more than transitory or symbolic power, and discipline is only a feature of warrior behaviour when they become captured by the State, and are transformed into a military order. As in Bataille, the military order is the war-impulse as appropriated by the real-world logic of the State. In this form in both arguments, it becomes a violence turned against itself, thus both repressing and intensifying itself. In this way, its logic is classically economic in the Freudian sense, generating that which undermines it, animating colliding impulses in the form of one another. It is an example of the complex arrangements that are necessary to the State-apparatus, and that defy the simple logic of interiority and exteriority on which State thinking normally relies.

In short, there is no simple inside and outside to the State. The State operates by way of its complex endorsement and encouragement of that which it ostensibly reviles and that defies it. These putative antagonists to the State maintain their hostility and defiance, seeking implicitly in every facet of their operation to defy and dismantle the State, while they are used for its advancement. They bring an impossible logic to the heart of the State itself, where it develops only by way of that which frustrates it, and advances by way of the operation of that which it would seek to surpass:

> The State itself has always been in a relation with an outside and is inconceivable independent of that relationship. The law of the State is not the law of All or Nothing (State societies *or* counter-State societies) but that of interior and exterior. The State is sovereignty. But sovereignty only reigns over what it is capable of internalising, of appropriating locally...The outside appears simultaneously in two directions: huge worldwide machines branched out over the entire *ecumenon* at a given moment, which enjoy a large measure of autonomy in relation to the States...but also the local mechanisms of bands, margins, minorities, which continue to affirm the rights of segmentary societies in opposition to the organs of State power...These directions are equally present in all social fields, in all periods. It even happens that they partially merge. For example, a commercial organisation is also a band of pillage, or piracy, for part of its course and in many of its activities; or it is in bands that a religious organisation begins to operate...It is in terms not of independence, but of coexistence and competition *in a perpetual field of interaction*, that we must conceive of exteriority and interiority, war machines of metamorphosis and State apparatuses of identity, bands and kingdoms, megamachines and empires.
>
> (Deleuze and Guattari, 1987, pp. 360–1)

The State demands that there be something exterior to itself that contradicts its logic and thus validates its right to legislate. The daylight logic of the State must own the contrary culture of the segmented within its own universality. Presenting this relationship as an ordered contradiction allows the State to validate itself, by locating the war-machine as its logical other, on whose back it can step in order to reach a higher synthetic ascendancy. Yet this logic is itself a device to simplify, to *represent*, a relationship that is far more complicated, in which the violent war-machine advances itself by turning on itself in service of that which legislates its mutilation. Beneath every operation of the State, then, we find the things that confuse and defy it intensifying and developing it at the same time. The State has no other means of operation, and can only legalise its own alien monsters. The empire relies on the mercenaries that will both fight for it and extend its borders and ultimately risk its essence. The State and the war-machine require this kind of intense imbrication in one another, despite how they represent themselves. We have then a double operation: the State cannot move without harnessing the logic of metamorphosis and violence that defies it; the war-machine merely blows away in the wind unless at some point it institutes some moment of some State. The State unleashes the war-machine and then erases it, except as the laughable long-surpassed and suppressed primitive; the war-machine appears only in and through the State and would be invisible otherwise. Like the logic of intimacy and the real which appeal to and generate one another, the war-machine and the State make sense only together.

As in Bataille, the military order is the denomination of this togetherness that struggles to deny the complexity and instability of this relationship. Yet it remains a war-machine. Like many of the collective bodies that hover round and within the State, it is unstable, sometimes demonstrating its collaboration with hierarchy, discipline and order, even deploying violence in service of order, at other times threatening to reveal its native scepticism towards the State, as something that perplexes it, even when it is in its service. In this way it is emblematic of all the bodies that the State requires: sometimes docile and conservative, but also hiding the possibility of a breakout that will release "in unforeseen forms" (Deleuze and Guattari, 1987, p. 366) the cataclysmic logic of the war-machine. This is not because these bodies incarnate a simple self-contradictory double logic, where they sometimes conform to the logic of the State and sometimes to its alternative. It is because they unearth, from within the State, that element of it that resists it, that mounts *violence contra violence*, that in the intensification of its loyalty to the State accelerates betrayal.

The State then can only survive by entrusting itself to its own failure. Deleuze and Guattari plot this complex relationship in terms of conceptual thought. In its aspiration to the universal, conceptual thought "borrows" a model from the State apparatus "which defines for it goals and paths, conduits, channels, organs, an entire organon" (Deleuze and Guattari, 1987, p. 374). Like the State, thought has twin figure-heads. One operates by "magical capture" (p. 374), establishing by the throwing out, the projection of a ground, a foundation on which practice can arise, a mythos, in other words. The other institutes laws and conventions on this basis, constructing an elaborate and contractual civilisation of arrangements, a parliament of practices, in other words, a logos (pp. 374–5). Yet these two operate only if there is something that electrifies the gap between them and makes the ether move. The State then cannot go on only and indefinitely hymning stasis. It must shift, break or undo itself somehow, otherwise it cannot live in and through the time it claims to know. This threat of the State to itself can be traced through a history that represents scientific break-through in avant-garde terms: the artistic tastes of scientists, their self-mutilating experiments upon themselves, the cult of inexplicable uneducable genius, and their appalling dress-sense. The moment of scientific innovation is suppressed behind the inexplicable blur of radical, creative thought.

Thought itself is an exteriority that resists the systematisation of the universal conceptualisation that collaborates with and sustains the State. In this way, the moment of inventive thought itself is invisible to conceptual and historical logic, and is rationalised by romantic tropes such as genius or inspiration, even in science. Deleuze and Guattari refer to Artaud's account of thought as a "central breakdown," that "lives solely by its own incapacity to take on form, bringing into relief only traits of expression in a material, developing peripherally, in a pure milieu of exteriority, as a function of singularities impossible to universalise, of circumstances impossible to interiorise" (Deleuze and Guattari, 1987, p. 378). Thought then unsettles, problematises and preserves some trace of its outlaw, forbidden origins:

> A thought grappling with exterior forces instead of being gathered up in an interior form, operating by relays instead of forming an image; an event-thought, a haecceity, instead of a subject-thought, a problem-thought instead of an essence-thought or theorem; a thought that appeals to a people instead of taking itself for a government ministry.
>
> (Deleuze and Guattari, 1987, p. 378)

"The classical image of thought" (p. 379) implicitly refers to the totality of the conceptual whole, the Absolute or the universe, the ultimate principle or the unifying theory, as grasped by a unified Subject. Nomad thought, on the other hand, betrays universal thinking for the horizonless adventure, and is grounded in loyalty to the singular race, not the subject individual (p. 379). This race, Deleuze and Guattari hasten to explain, is not defined by its purity or by its dominance, but by its minoritarian position as oppressed and alien to the conformist logic of the State. The tribe race is not defined by the abstract and interior conceptual and thus State logic of its bloodlines, but by its shared habitation of undefined, smooth space. This race then is one of transient alliances and experimental collaborations inventing itself as a necessary part of its complication and interrogation of the real. In Deleuze and Guattari's description, thought lets itself down into conceptualisation as both that which makes it possible and that which disturbs it. Conceptualisation is the permanence of thought, its attempt to sink into the language, structure and order that the State requires. Yet thought has its origins in a disturbance of the real, a disruption that conceptualisation must both draw on and obscure. This obscuring takes the form of a romantic mystification, an evocation of the unrepresentable as the almost magical flash that separates one respected continent of thought from its unforeseen successor. The State then strives to obscure and rationalise the nomad, war-machine logic on which it depends.

The State then does not simply supersede the war-machine as a more advanced form that captures and subordinates it. It reinvents the war-machine as part of or after itself. This reinvention can take the form of the dissent and radicalism it provokes as its necessary antagonist, that it continually strives to control and subdue, but also the horizonless expansions that are the inevitable by-product of its own will to self-aggrandisement. The State seeks to reorganise smooth nomad space so that it becomes like its own rationalised, striated space. Yet this will to know, own and map all space cannot be totally controlled. It produces an extroversion that overspills the State's ability to reduce and map it. Para-State phenomena, in enlarging the provenance of the State, inevitably reopen and wander into a space that is unmappable and unknown, reinventing themselves as war-machines, as ephemeral and experimental, in a "new nomadism" which "accompanies a worldwide war-machine whose organisation exceeds the State apparatuses and passes into energy, military-industrial and multinational complexes" (Deleuze and Guattari, 1987, p. 387). The State does not enclose nomadism, no matter what it says. Despite its logic of limits, boundaries and definitions, the State is open to the nomadism that feeds it and also to the nomadism it may subtend, as the inevitable exhaustion of its capacity to control is confronted. Importantly, as Deleuze and Guattari remind us here, the disruption and experimentalism of the nomadic is not to be understood naively or romantically as simply preferable to the order of the State. It may be no less violent, appropriative or destructive, perhaps even more so.

Yet again, it is important for us to remind ourselves that what is at stake is not the evaluation of one alternative against another, but the understanding of and management of the complex immersion of the war-machine and the State in one another. The State and the war-machine defy and refute one another, but at the same time, they transmute one into the other, remain open to one another even as they refuse one another, and so on. The war-machine is sucked into the operation of the State, as the latter maps and encloses smooth space. Yet, the offices instituted by the State overspill the criss-cross taxonomies of State logic seeking adventure, and transmuting into war-machines themselves. Or alternatively, the State provokes self-destructive gangs, doomed to a fatal liberation through crime, intoxication or abuse. Rioters torch their own suburbs, victims cut their own skin, children adore the doctor who tortures them: the wilderness culture of the steppes is reawoken in slums, amongst artists and academics in an unabashed senselessness that refuses the logic of rule, in a pointless, automatic dissent. In turn, from this danger, purpose grows: a marketable brand of street-wear, a no longer quite so outlaw popular music, a government subsidy for the exhibition of avant-garde art and so on. Yet this optimistic appropriation should not hide from us the fact of real danger, and the real distrust between these antagonists who require one another. Even as they form uneasy co-ordinations, they really threaten one another.

This complex inter-relationship means that the same item may function differently depending on the context in which it is used, yet without becoming two different things. This idea emerges in Deleuze and Guattari's discussion of the ambiguous status of the implement that could be a tool in one formation or a weapon in another. What distinguishes them is not the intrinsic nature of the thing itself, but the assemblage into which they are integrated. This assemblage is not to be seen in purely mechanical or material terms, however, as the announced and planned design of a certain social institution. A complex set of theoretical variables allows the specificity of the assemblage to be understood—"...[its] direction (projection-introception), [its] vector (speed-gravity), [its] model (free action-work), [its] expression (jewellery-signs), and [its] passional or desiring tonality (affect-feeling)" (Deleuze and Guattari, 1987, p. 402). What is important is that the implement is a pivot around which the complex economy war-machine/State revolves:

> There is a schizophrenic taste for the tool that moves it away from work and toward free action, a schizophrenic taste for the weapon that turns it into a means for peace, for obtaining peace. A counter-attack and a resistance simultaneously. Everything is ambiguous...The borrowing

between warfare and the military apparatus, work and free action, always run in both directions, for a struggle that is all the more varied.
(Deleuze and Guattari, 1987, p. 403)

The military apparatus is a particularly intense site of this complicated relationship (p. 404). Deleuze and Guattari go to some length to outline the complex economic relationships that underpin the double inspiration/desecration of the State/war-machine complex: "to the formed or formable matter we must add an entire energetic materiality in movement, carrying singularities or haecceities that are already like implicit forms that are topological, rather than geometrical, and that combine with processes of deformation" (Deleuze and Guattari, 1987, p. 408). It is worth remembering that the war-machine always seems the preferred model in such theorising because the State does not countenance movement and transformation except as an accident, and therefore seeks to deny or subordinate the war-machine on which it needs to draw. It is the unruly servant hidden in the basement on whom the whole running of the house depends. Any theorising that acknowledges the war-machine, even if it sees it as inseparable from the State, will always discomfort the State, and draw its repression.

How are we to understand the State/war-machine complex in its specific relation to war itself? For Deleuze and Guattari, war is not to be seen as a mere development from an undifferentiated "non-specific" natural violence (Deleuze and Guattari, 1987, p. 417), as it has been so commonly theorised. What exactly is the relationship between the war-machine and war? It is simply not enough to draw attention to the contrast between the commitment to grand strategy and the massing of matériel on the part of the State, its preference for battle, on the one hand, and, on the other hand, guerrilla warfare—a classic mode of the war-machine—which does all it can to avoid battle, or to be more accurate, to win victory through the complex dissemblings, lures and hit-and-run attacks that can be called non-battle (p. 416). The drive of the war-machine is to spread over smooth territory. It only fights war when it comes into collision with the State that wants to organise space in an opposing way. War, then, is not an expression of the inner essence of the war-machine, as much as the operation into which it extends when it is challenged. War is the consequence or culmination of the war-machine, rather than its fundamental nature. War and the war-machine are, in Kantian terms, in a synthetic, not analytic, relationship (p. 417).

Nor, on the other hand, is war an expression of the internal essence of the State. The State learnt war from the war-machine, and one of the most important questions in history is "how will the State appropriate the war-machine?" (Deleuze and Guattari, 1987, p. 418). The military apparatus is not the war-machine in itself, but is the latter as the State has appropriated it. It is in fact through this appropriation that the war-machine becomes straitened and disciplined, defined enough to have an object and purpose, war itself. It is not the war-machine itself, but the war-machine in conjunction with the State that displays dedication to war. This combination between the State and the war-machine proves lethal to the war-machine that remains on its own. The war-machine that has not learnt to work with the State is unable to solve the problems that victory proposes in terms of how conquered territory should be organised or even known. In this way, the war-machine that the State turns back on the nomad will always prove victorious in the long-run. The war-machine is in fact threatened by its complex relation to itself and its commitment to expansiveness and adventure in the face of success and gain, which propose problems that require an answer that cannot simply be distilled from the war-machine itself. Victory brings the encounter with fixity and defines movement in relation to fixities. Adventure becomes migration. Supply requires support: "the elements of nomadism...enter into de facto mixes with elements of migration, itinerancy, and transhumance; this does not effect the purity of the concept, but introduces always mixed objects, or combinations of space and composition, which react back upon the war-machine from the beginning" (Deleuze and Guattari, 1987, p. 420). The war-machine is always subject to the possibility of settlement, "thus the integration of the nomad into the State is a vector traversing nomadism from the very beginning, from the first act of war against the State" (p. 420).

Similarly, the method used by the State to subordinate the war-machine to State-purposes and meaning remains always problematic for the State. We have seen above how the State appropriates and subsumes nomadic logic, marshalling and harnessing it, but that then, the institutions of the State overspill the constraints of State logic to reinvent themselves as war-machines. The same thing happens specifically in relation to war. The State appropriates the war-machine and gives it war as its set object. Because of its universalising thinking and its commitment to finality, the State always drives to transform its war-machine into total war. This links State war to capitalism, according to Deleuze and Guattari, because only capitalism can provide the resources that make total war possible. Furthermore, in total war, the social and its future change from being a mere resource to being the meaning and purpose of war. Alternative societies in total war are not merely to be subdued but annihilated. In this sense, total war "merely realizes the maximal conditions of the appropriation of the war machine by the State apparatus" (Deleuze and Guattari, 1987, p. 421).

But unconditioned war is itself always a threat to the State, not only the States it targets but the State that seeks to put it into operation. Once warfare has become unlimited, with an absolute object, then the State is itself encountering its limits and flirting with the perilous game of trying to put them into operation. The State has given rise to a worldwide war-machine to which it increasingly becomes subordinate. "the appropriation has changed direction, or rather that States tend to unleash, reconstitute, an immense war-machine of which they are no longer anything more than the opposable or apposed parts" (Deleuze and Guattari, 1987, p. 421). The war-machine then encompasses the whole earth, and exceeds the States that have chosen it. This remapping of the planet by a war-machine in excess of the State was, in Deleuze and Guattari's hands, a way of describing in a new way a world under threat of Mutually Assured Destruction, during the Cold War. However, it is worth considering this in terms of the War On Terror, which has equally held the world hostage to a war-machine perhaps impossible to control. "[I]t is necessary to follow the real movement at the conclusion of which the States, having appropriated a war machine, and having adapted it to their aims, reimpart a war machine that takes charge of the aim, appropriates the States, and assumes increasingly wider political functions" (Deleuze and Guattari, 1987, p. 421). The war on terror unleashes a total war-machine that overflows the logic of the State and that the State is unable to control. In turn, the culture of the State, its commitment to identity, citizenship and order are under threat from the impulse to violence and domination ostensibly used to protect the State. Because it does not recognise responsibility, the war-machine, even when the State believes it has it under control in the institution of the military order, cannot be held accountable. As we have seen in Freud and Bataille, the inclusion of this logic within the State always means that the military order can so easily slip over into atrocity. It also means that the imperative of war can be used to evade the normal constitutional restraints of civil society: the culture of war brings into politics a violence and desperation protected from legal niceties like civil rights by a sentimental and physical crudeness and impatience that over-rides the subtleties of law, and even the discussion of political priorities. We must pay attention to the gravity of generals. We must support the troops no matter how cynical or absurd is the war in which they are prepared to fight.

There are other, perhaps more phantasmatic, ways in which the war-machine redefines the State. For example, in entertainment, politics becomes subordinate to a kind of lust, in which the State becomes the mere nominal shell of a visceral violence. A teenager secretly refights the Gulf War. He wins a faster, a simpler victory this time, purging his country's purpose of any complication or hesitation. He can ignore all nagging voices. So pure, so patriotic, so uncompromising, so intent, so meaningful, so violent is his trajectory, the parliamentary, bureaucratic, media-savvy sophistries that the State itself has to negotiate cannot inhibit him. There is a clean, vicious, notable and unironic splendour in his violence that he feels he needs to hide, even though he is proud of it. He is more merciless, more purposeful, more right than even the righteousness he commemorates. Folded into his glory is the validation of the victory of his nation and the carnal luxury of the cruelty it licenses but cannot publicly enact. His mission is a daylight validation of the troops but lacks the conscience and constraint, and the reason to be right. So, his dirty war is a dirty secret he keeps from even himself. Bodies fly backwards over his head, uncounted, unnamed, an ill-defined yet maniacal vermin, easily forgotten. Even the righteous victory of the missionary State played out in your darkened room is shameful: a bit too unrestrained, a bit too cruel, a bit more than might be necessary. The licence provided by the victorious State validates but chokes the cruel subterfuge of the vicious righteous child.

The hot cathexis of national solidity ensures the President of inalienable righteousness. From here on in, it is all just planning and persuasion. He knows it can only end well. Even cruelty and subterfuge are allowed, perhaps even enjoyed in the confirmation of righteousness. Who can stop us? Force and then success excuse everything, creating realities on the ground that must be accepted. Who then can say they are better than us when we have won? There is no logic of empire, just aggrandisement, the meaningfulness of more, of stronger, of wilder, of FREEDOM. No one can take it away. The point is that even when it is validated by the higher reason of the State, even when it is suppressed into the strict lineaments of the military apparatus, even when there is a liberalism, a humanism, a liberation, a democracy, a rationalism, an idealism, human rights, a coherent academic argument, a law, a justice, a discourse of gender equity, national progress, human meaning and so on and so forth, it is always a violence unleashing cruelty, righteousness, calumny, honour, intimidation, sentimentality, brutality and all the other logics of the rampant war-machine, the war-machine and reason allowing, excusing, validating, concealing one another.

How does the fighting child connect with the righteous president, the pondering general, the ambitious journalist and the anxious activist? They play out a meaningful give and take where different levels of decision validate one another. The hidden lineaments of the fighting boy may or may not feed the hard calculation of the president; the heroic worldliness of the soldier may or may not require the president's duty of cynical care, but draws on it, and is *released* by it anyway. What lies behind the decisions that get made, what memories? What traces? What trust in now or never, now and forever? What lusts are in question? Something gives us energy, faith, hope, trust, where does it come from if not the unleashing of the disruptive energy of rebuilding to which our violence is committed? In other words, we are doing it now. The double logic of the war-machine and the State run through the social body, the way it twists in on itself, choosing and unchoosing the violence that brings both order and freedom, in our politics, in our diplomacy, in our social vision, in our relationships and in our entertainment, all enfolded in and over one another, refusing, frustrating and feeding on one another. The war that appals us, that we conjure as the forever last resort, defies all of our values, but it also reassures us, flatters us and frees us, and we trust it. The order that we implement is the consolidation of the energy of disruption, harm, movement and self-mutilation we revile, and, in turn, only order requires movement. It will not end, this feeding and folding over of that which despises multiplies and alienates itself. It will never be over.

Under the black light: Derrida, Levinas, Schmitt and the aporia of war

As we have seen, the war/other complex, or the "economic" model of the war/other relationship, understands the metaphysical not as the primary or over-arching principles by which explanations can be formulated and evaluations made. Instead, it usually allocates metaphysics a specific location within the complex, which thus both makes metaphysics possible and exceeds it. In this sense, war unfolds through a set of complex relationships where meaning and identity are themselves under question. The destination of this way of thinking about war, then, is implicitly deconstructive. The consequences are that war itself can never be stabilised into a fixed and discrete identity, and must be understood not in terms of a set of knowable and manageable relationships with its others, but in aporetic entanglements with them. In such entanglements, the frontier between what is war and what is not is always unclear, and the definitions of both war and its others remain irreducibly problematic. In pragmatic political terms, this means that the relationship between war and its other must be constantly renegotiated, in the Derridean sense of negotiation as the constant management of the political consequences of the irresolution of identities. We cannot take refuge in the sentimental idea of an achievable perpetual peace, while at the same time we cannot simply resign ourselves to the idea that war is either inevitable, productive or meaningful. Let us now turn to Derrida's deconstructive or aporetic account of war.

Derrida's reading of the political theory of Carl Schmitt in *The Politics of Friendship* takes place under the sign of a tribute by Derrida to Nietzsche's aim "to show the ineluctable necessity of this perversion which made opposites pass into one another; the friend into the enemy, the strong into the weak, the hegemonic into the oppressed and so forth" (Derrida, 1997, p. 80). Such a way of thinking could not have been the preserve or product of an individual thinker, according to Derrida, but reflects a mutation to which "we" belong (p. 80), one that sends a tremor through the very notion of belonging itself, in all possible versions of social combination. "We belong to this tremor, if that is possible; we tremble within it" (p. 80). This complication destabilises the destiny of thought itself by introducing irreducible aporias into a logic which prefers conclusiveness. "We wish only to think that we are on the track of an impossible axiomatic which remains to be thought" (p. 81). The aporia complicates and frustrates thinking, but no worthwhile conclusion is attainable without it. What could be thought without a thorough engagement with this difficulty? "Almost nothing," Derrida concludes. A political history or theory that understood itself as extra-discursive and teleological "would deck itself out in 'realism' just in time to fall short of the thing—and to repeat, repeat and repeat again, with neither consciousness nor memory of its compulsive droning" (p. 81).

If we are to understand the account of war that emerges in Derrida's readings of Levinas and Schmitt, we must embrace the challenge of this aporetic logic in which like and unlike "pass into" one another. We have seen in Bataille how war and civic realism generate one another in their clash and recoil from one another. In the economy of war, war and peace cannot be seen to be in simple contradiction with one another, nor as fundamentally separate. War and peace provoke and generate one another even as they abominate one another. Here, there is no war without peace and no peace without war. In Derrida, the argument goes further. The distinctions on which the definition of war and peace are seen to depend—the distinction between friend and enemy, for example—are seen to be untenable. War and peace endure in one another. Friendship and enmity combine in multiple overlaps and inter-penetrations.

If war and peace cannot be kept sensibly apart, are we to abandon attempts to minimise war in historical and political terms, on the one hand, and to try and think human society without it, on the other? There are two consequences to this deconstruction of the war/peace binary, one pragmatic, the other theoretical. Derrida's philosophy of political pragmatism does not rely on the rigid separation between alternatives, but the patient and thorough "negotiation" of a path through options whose identity or separation from one another can never be taken for granted. This negotiation requires attention to the specific and unique context in which the war/peace problem arises. Similarly, it requires the kind of open practice of decision that Derrida has written about extensively, a decision always open to the indeterminate, and thus always involving a taking-on of responsibility.

In theoretical terms, what this deconstruction requires is a rethinking of the usefulness of the terms "war" and "peace." Indeed, in Derrida's discussion of Schmitt's trope of "the real possibility of war," we will see how war's significance is not a cruel and violent material event as much as the bullying logic by which social life is defined. War is first and foremost a problem for the idea of society. Material violence is secondary to this. We know how wars can be fought without being declared, without crossing the conceptual or legal threshold that allows them to be proclaimed, or owned, as war. This means that there is a dissociation between fighting that we may understand as unambiguously warfare and the use of the term. The idea and practice of war are not one and the same thing. The consequence of this is that what we know to be wars are fought without being called war, and the term itself is most forcefully applied to administer, control, dampen and intimidate the opening of the social itself. If the key function of the concept of war has been—since Hobbes—to discipline social life, then we cannot take refuge in the strong opposition between war and peace. If the main function of the concept of war is to rule peace, then peace itself is a concept we must do without. The nature of sociality itself must be rethought.

Derrida's thought on war emerges through a reading of Levinas and of Schmitt. Let us look at these one at a time. What is war to Levinas? "The visage of being that shows itself in war is fixed in the concept of totality" (Levinas, 1969, p. 21), Levinas writes in the Preface to *Totality and Infinity*. It later emerges that this is not to be taken to mean that war is simply totality—the summary logic of system, completion and the self-same—as historical player. War is not simply an expression of the total, as much as it is the sundering of beings locked in the logic of totality: "it destroys the identity of the same" (p. 21) even as it seems to rely on it, develop from it and be animated by it. War then is not the incarnation of the limiting logic of totality as much as that logic in its breakdown. War is not the setting of limited beings against one another simply because of the limit that divides them:

> War cannot be derived from the empirical fact of the multiplicity of beings that limit one another, under the pretext that where the presence of the one inevitably limits the other, violence is identical with this limitation. Limitation is not of itself violence.
> (Levinas, 1969, p. 222)

Levinas is locating his work right at the heart of an historical moment. War is the first theme he discusses in *Totality and Infinity* and he returns to it, not to abominate it, nor to find another reason to anathematise its culture and motives, nor to claim an authority or wisdom because of what he has suffered (and he has suffered), but instead to *risk* his whole philosophy, to hold in check the benign authoritarianism of the redemption it might mistakenly seem simply to offer. Perhaps he is afraid of his philosophy and needs to reel it in, to hold it back, and by holding it back, bringing it closer and closer to that which it suspects and challenges, locate it here and now with us, not somewhere of which we might only dream. Violence, you see, is not simply a result of the logic of totality—how tempting would it have been given the shadow of totalitarianism over the politics of the immediately previous period to have simply said that! Instead he says, "Violence in nature...refers to an existence precisely not limited by an other, an existence that maintains itself outside of the totality" (Levinas, 1969, p. 222). Violence exceeds totality. Violence connects with what sunders the self-identity of the limited subject. It is not part of the logic of self-identity, but of what brings it undone. Indeed, what is conventionally called peace is not peace, but the mere "exclusion of violence" (p. 222). There is a simple and nominal, but not real and enduring, peace under the logic of totality. True peace only really arises at the point where totality is exceeded, in the form of "the eschatology of messianic peace...[coming]...to superpose itself upon the ontology of war" (p. 22). War then resides at the point where totality breaks down and opens itself to the eschatology and the infinity that will bring some messianic peace. War and peace touch one another at the point of the opening of totality onto infinity and of ontology onto eschatology. Levinas writes, "Only beings capable of war can rise to peace. War like peace presupposes beings structured otherwise than as parts of a totality" (p. 222). Again "War...presupposes[s] the face and the transcendence of the being appearing in the face" (p. 222).

In war, the limited self-identity of beings, which would seem to allow them to be mere fractions of a totality, breaks up. This break-up makes war more than a mere confirmation of a totality. War is an instance of the opening of that which exceeds totality. This, in turn, is what opens war to peace. Peace then is not a stable ideal system compatible with the logic of totality or law and order. Peace is not the mere settling of limited beings into the jigsaw totality that would accommodate them as cohabiting parts of a single meaningful whole. Peace is not the respect of a limited being for another limited being to whom it might agree to relinquish the sovereignty of an adjacent space, a respect you might expect to be reciprocated. The very opening up of limited beings to the eschatology, or the infinity that exceeds them, an opening up that, as we have seen, is necessary to violence, is also the opening of something that is the possibility of real peace, a peace that is more than the mere exclusion of violence. What makes war possible is what makes peace possible. Peace exceeds war, but not by simply opposing it. War opens in the same dimension and in the same direction as peace, indeed, under its auspices, as part of its operation. Like totality itself, which is conditioned by infinity (Levinas, 1969, p. 24) and could not emerge separate from it, war is cultivated by the peace that must supersede and thus defeat it.

Derrida discusses the entanglement of war and peace, as it pertains to Levinas, in *Adieu: To Emmanuel Levinas*. "What is peace?" he asks (Derrida, 1999, p. 85). Talk of peace only makes sense in relation to a welcoming of the other. There can be no peace in sameness. What would be the point? Since within the logic of sameness, or non-difference, no separation is possible, how could there be the disjunction that would require reconciliation and peace? Does this mean that sameness is the classical space of war? No, Derrida argues. It is not the case that, on the one hand, we have peace and otherness, and, on the other, war and sameness. "War and peace are...too often thought to form a symmetrical pair of opposed concepts" (Derrida, 1999, p. 86). We should not automatically assume that war and peace are opposites or even perhaps mutually exclusive.

The fallacy of opposing war to peace is particularly problematic when one of these terms is credited with being prior or even originary: "give to one or the other of these two concepts a value or position of originarity, and the symmetry is broken" (p. 86). The mainstream of the

Western political tradition from Hobbes through Kant to the Patriot Act assumes the social as an invention whose aim is not necessarily to foreclose a strictly demarcated real historical period of war by instituting and institutionalising a social peace in all ways and everywhere legal, consensual and ordered, but to at least ward off the perpetual recurrence of violence always pressing in from the imaginary outside of society. Derrida summarises the Kantian version of this argument, tellingly. Kant "thinks...that everything in nature begins with war" (p. 86). Kant's view has two corollaries. First, peace is not merely a part of a natural double with war, in which they exist as necessarily and inevitably as one another, a nature in which there has obviously always been war just as easily as there has always been peace. Instead, peace is an institution. It is of "a non-natural nature" (p. 86). Second, it must be a positive phenomenon, not merely the absence of violence. It must arise as a new world for humanity, something unheard of before and raising our hopes and eyes to the horizon of an altogether new possibility.

So peace must be a positive phenomenon, not separable and opposable to war, but something instituted within, after and because of war as the invention of the possibility of the enduring and optimistic social accommodation we make in relation to one another. There must be then a disjunction between war and peace, even as they depend on one another. They cannot collaborate. The cessation of hostility as a tactic, the decision to call a halt to war because this might lead to some political or diplomatic advantage is not peace, but merely a strategy of war without explicit fighting. So the relationship between war and peace cannot lead simply to the argument that powers use peace as a tactic in a perpetual war that robs the concept of peace of any meaning. Undoubtedly they do, but we cannot simply hide in an automatic and exasperated cynicism, implying that we expect nothing better from the world.

According to Derrida, Levinas adopts the contrary position to Kant:

> Whereas for Kant the institution of an eternal peace, of a cosmopolitical law, and of a universal hospitality, retains the trace of a natural hostility, whether present or threatening, real or virtual, for Levinas, the contrary would be so: war itself retains the testimonial trace of a pacific welcoming of the face.
>
> (Derrida, 1999, p. 88)

Neither Kant nor Levinas's position then can be seen to endorse the idea of a simple symmetrical opposition between war and peace. For one, peace appears in a social landscape already marked out and fully occupied by war, interrupting, supplanting and in the end withstanding it. That is because this peace then is defined by the war it is contrived to deal with, and therefore always bears with it some trace of war. The second, Levinasian view, sees war as emerging as a denial or concealment of a peace larger than and prior to it. These ideas in turn are not symmetrical because they come from different domains. Kant's peace is legal and political; his war is notionally historical. On the other hand, Levinas's peace is metaphysical and his war ontological. This is important, because if peace in Kant is always reminiscent of war, then we cannot really hope for much more from it than what Derrida calls an "armed peace" (Derrida, 1999, p. 91). For Derrida, Levinas:

> breaks with both Kant and Hegel, with both a juridico-cosmopolitanism that, in spite of its claims to the contrary, could never succeed in interrupting an armed peace, peace as armistice, and with the laborious process—the work—of the negative, 'with a peace process' that would still organise war by other means when it does not make of it a condition of consciousness, of 'objective morality' (*Sittlichkeit*) and of politics.
>
> (Derrida, 1999, p. 91)

What Levinas holds out is the possibility of a peace without war, perhaps irreducibly distant, but a peace without a trace of war nonetheless, admittedly an eschatological peace, but one in touch with the always already open face of the Other, a peace then, to which war will always be something junior.

War, on the other hand, will never be without a trace of peace. Peace will always have priority over war, and war will always carry with it a trace of the peace it cannot finally and absolutely surpass. It is a way of thinking of a peace without war, but a war that can never be without peace:

> [W]ar, hostility, even murder, still presuppose and thus always manifest this originary welcoming that is openness to the face...One can make war only against a face: one can kill, or give oneself the prohibition not to kill, only where the epiphany of the face has taken place, even if one rejects, forgets, or denies it in an allergic reaction.
>
> (Derrida, 1999, p. 90)

Peace then always shows up war. One can only kill that thing that has opened itself to you in a revelation of a primordial peace. Peace will always exceed your act of killing.

Yet, despite its assertion of the primacy of peace, there is a horror to this logic. Even killing here is notionally peaceful, despite itself. Peace has pre-defeated war, by being something that can subsist before and without it. But this victory might not make any difference. Peace has the last laugh on war by contaminating war and redeeming it, even though it remains war, by insinuating itself into a killing that it then mitigates and destabilises. According to this logic, people may still be dead, but what killed them was residually peaceful. The violence I commit on you is actually the vehicle of a peaceful purpose it would seem to contradict, but that very peace is actually its meaning. The meaning of the violence I bring to you is democracy, inevitably, and automatically, without my actually having to make peace and democracy more than traces.

In Levinasian philosophy, subjectivity itself is always already open onto otherness when it comes into existence. Whatever the subject does cannot erase the priority of otherness. Usually, this is sentimentalised: liberal individualism in its selfishness and solipsism is revealed to be chimerical, because the individual can only be instituted in relation to a prior other, even though it might deny this. Yet here we have something more ambiguous. The subject's violence also remains an enactment of the subject's relationship to the other. War is always haunted by the peace it would seem to abolish. Peace will not be annihilated. This may mean that a thin thread of peace endures the cruelty of war, waiting to be recovered, reasserted and restored when hostilities lessen.

Above all, however, it means that war always remains a social act, even in its viciousness. Sociality never merely supersedes or excludes war as it does for Hobbes and Kant. Nor is there anywhere in Levinas where war and peace are continuous with one another, as they are for Clausewitz and Foucault. Here the entanglement of war and peace reaches a deeper level. We have seen how with Freud, Bataille and Deleuze/Guattari, war and its other arise in relationship to one another, provoking, challenging and producing one another. In Levinas, the relationship is even closer: war is the trace of peace. The two are suspended in the smallest possible separation from one another. They hesitate on the verge of becoming identical. If sociality is the enactment of the prior relationship to the other, then war is the problem of the social. To deal with this complex non-identity of war and peace, the social must be experienced, not as the potential wealth of human mutual enhancement, recoverable from behind the narcissism of liberal individualism, but always and everywhere a problem.

Derrida provides two other ways of complicating the relationship between war and peace in his critique of Carl Schmitt in *Politics of Friendship*. One involves the complication of the friend/enemy distinction, on which

Schmitt's concept of the political depends. The other is his reading of Schmitt's definition of the social in terms of "the real possibility of war" as a style of spectrality. I want to consider these one at a time.

As is well known, Schmitt defines the political in terms of the possibility of enmity. For Schmitt, what gives me an identity as a member of a social group is the identification of the enemy and the "determined possibility of an actual war" (Derrida, 1997, p. 84) with him or her. According to Schmitt, this enmity is not the result of personal antipathy, or even of a group antagonism traceable to historical causes, such as rivalry over land, water or access to resources. Nor is it motivated by something to do with the identity of the enemy, such as their ethnicity, or their membership of a particular cultural, class or religious group. It may, of course, take this form, as a way of simplifying or representing real political arrangements, but it is not because of their ethnicity that a particular ethnic group is my enemy. It is because I need an enemy, and defining it using some simple obvious marker of identity is easy, but the enmity itself is structural, and not motivated by anything in particular about the enemy. Enmity of this kind, therefore, has no psychological or even cultural weight at all, other than as pretext or propaganda. Enmity does not flow from a psychological need, on either an individual or a collective basis. It is simply a requirement that if one is to have politics, it must be on the basis of identifying an enemy. Indeed, the more enmity is defined by personal antipathy or xenophobia, the less purely political it is.

If war can be waged without antipathy, then it can of course be waged on the friend. Derrida writes,

> the political enemy would not inevitably be inimical, he would not necessarily hold me in enmity, nor I him. Moreover, sentiments would play no role; there would be neither passion nor affect in general. Here we have a totally pure experience of the friend-enemy in its political essence, purified of any affect—at least of all personal affect, supposing that there could ever be any other kind. If the enemy is the stranger, the war I would wage on him should remain essentially without hatred, without intrinsic *xenophobia*. And politics would begin with this purification. With the calculation of this conceptual purification. I can also wage war on my friend, a war in the proper sense of the term, a proper, clear and merciless war. But a war without hatred.
> (Derrida, 1997, pp. 87–8)

Since there is no necessary connection between the personal nature of affection and the structural logic of hostility, there is no limit to who could be my enemy. My friend is not my enemy, but since affectivity is not an issue in my structural relationship with my enemy, my relationship with my friend does not preclude the possibility of him or her being my enemy as well. And at the same time, it is possible to have, therefore, a friend-enemy, who is the person with whom I have a personal friendship, but who is structurally the enemy of the political group to which I belong. According to this logic, it would be possible for someone to be not just your friend who becomes your enemy, but to be completely and thoroughly both your friend and your enemy at one and the same time.

This conundrum can easily be solved by insisting on the strict separation between public and private, and Derrida argues that Schmitt's discourse is absolutely reliant on the stability of this dichotomy (Derrida, 1997, p. 88). The use of this distinction, however, is complicated by the fact that the concept of the "public," of the coherent and formed social group, appears here twice, in different places. The public is constituted by enmity, but the nature of this enmity, the fact that it is social and structural, and not personal and private, can only make sense if the notion of the public already exists. My personal friendships, then, cannot be separated from the public domain before that domain actually exists, yet that domain cannot come into existence without the separation having first taken place. In other words, the distinction between public and private can only arise in terms of enmity, but an enmity that itself can only exist if the distinction between public and private is already in place.

In this conundrum, the strict separation between personal friendship and public enmity becomes impossible, meaning that the enmity I might feel for my friend cannot be strictly separated from my love, because the domain that would allow the separation to take place cannot emerge prior to that separation. The consequence is that what Schmitt offers as the logic by which friendship and enmity can be conceptually distinguished fails to operate. Friendship and enmity cannot settle into the separate zones that would allow them to cohabit neatly. The frontier between them is permeable, and their relationship to one another—the relationship of relationship, in fact—will become irretrievably aporetic.

The complexity here is doubled by the fact that Schmitt insists on the European origin of this concept of the political. Derrida extrapolates from this to consider how enmity at the frontier of "civilisations" becomes, in this context, not just an enmity *within* the logic of the political, but between the civilisation of the logic of the political and other, therefore putatively non-political, civilisations. Derrida notes how Schmitt's example is a telling one for us, the millennium long conflict between Christianity and Islam:

> In question would be a defensive operation destined to defend *the* political, beyond particular states or nations, beyond any geographical, ethnic or political continent. On the political side of this unusual front, the stakes would be saving the political as such, ensuring its survival in the face of another who would no longer even be a political enemy but an enemy of *the* political—more precisely, a being radically alien to the political as such.
>
> (Derrida, 1997, p. 89)

This adds more complexity to the concept of the political. The enemy who defines your solidarity might not only be your political enemy, but also might come from outside politics. This enemy would be both political and non-political at the same time, which would really mean that the relationship of enmity between you is both political and non-political. Yet this enemy does not only come from outside politics, but is anti-political. They are your enemy and not your enemy, but they are also opposed to the whole concept of enmity, perhaps even the enemy of enmity. And, as we remember from above, they could, at least hypothetically, be your friend!

The complex relationship here between friendship and enmity not only undoes Schmitt's logic, but opens friendship and enmity onto one another till complex overlaps and multiplicities of the two become available in a potentially endless sequence. Friendship and enmity cannot be kept apart and can translate, even transmute one into another potentially without term. What this means is that Schmitt's attempt to ground the political in enmity fails because of the impurity, the impossible purity of that concept. If enmity emerges as a concept on which to ground a political distinction, it can only do so by insisting that its logical situation not be investigated. This means that enmity only works as a concept of the political by forcefully suppressing any acknowledgement of its inextricable entanglement with a friendship, from which it can never be clearly or definitively distinguished. In Levinasian terms, this is an instance of how there always remains a trace of peace in war that war consistently seeks to conceal. The rationale for war only becomes possible if that trace is suppressed. A brutal material example would be the contriving of ethnic wars between neighbours who may have lived together more or less unproblematically for centuries, a pattern common on the frontier between Islam and Christianity from the collapse of the Ottoman Empire and the Treaty of Lausanne through the Balkan Wars to Abu Ghraib. Communal cohabitation in villages across South-East Europe and Asia Minor is forgotten in the name of an antipathy presented as inevitable and traditional. Western entanglements in the most cynical episodes of Middle Eastern history—even to the point of support for Saddam Hussein and preparedness to rationalise away his atrocities—is a friendship erased in the name of a righteous enmity unaffected by the complexities of actually having no choice but to live in the historical world. Enmity is made to emerge as if friendship had never been possible.

The relationship between friend and enemy, therefore, is one of complex inter-penetration and overlap, while at the same time some distinction, even disjunction, remains in force. You can only be my friend if it is possible for me to kill you:

> Not only could I enter into a relationship of friendship only with a *mortal*, but I could love in friendship only a mortal at least exposed to so-called violent death—that is, exposed to being killed, *possibly by myself*.
>
> (Derrida, 1997, p. 122)

In other words, you can only be my friend if it is possible that you can also be my enemy.

On the other hand, however, this does not result in a pure collapse of difference between friendship and enmity. The two do not merely become indistinct from or even symmetrical to one another:

> What is true of the enemy (I can or I must kill you, and vice versa) is the very thing that suspends, annuls, overturns or, at the very least, represses, transfigures or sublimates friendship, which is therefore simultaneously the same (repressed) thing and *something altogether different*.
>
> (Derrida, 1997, p. 120)

Friendship and enmity therefore must both coincide with and threaten one another. The difference between them never disappears and there always remains a clash between them. They never form part of a settled system. Rather, they install within one another something that will forbid either concept from ever becoming pure, unconditional or directed in any unambiguous way. We have seen above in our discussion of Levinas the argument that peace emerges not in contradiction to war as its opposite, but as that which both precedes and exceeds war as the grounds that war must interrupt and what will in turn surpass war as a kind of messianic eschatology. War cannot suppress the peace it necessarily entails and that will emerge through and beyond it. Friendship and enmity are in a similar relationship, one in which they can not only coincide with one another (you can be thoroughly my enemy and my friend at one and the same time) but where they require one another. It is not only that you can be both my friend and my enemy at the same time, but you can only be my friend if you can at any time, also be my enemy. This installs not an homogeneity at the heart of the political, which depends on the friend/enemy distinction for its identity, according to Schmitt, but a clash, a collapse of difference that always remains double. It is perhaps this doubleness that Freud explained by subjectifying it, as psychological ambivalence.

Derrida also succeeds in giving this complex structure of non-identity a political meaning when he deconstructs the opposition between inter-State and civil war, on which Schmitt relies. The friend/enemy distinction seeks to turn any struggle into a clash between State-like actors or two forms of the State. This means that a civil war must be reappraised as a war between two versions of the State, one actual and one either incipient or possible. Yet Derrida shows that "the prevailing determination of civil war in this analysis" (Derrida, 1997, p. 121) undercuts the friend/enemy distinction by collapsing it into a competition between co-citizens. The consequence of this for our argument is that the economy of friendship and enmity that we have identified above is not only one that complicates—forms and also threatens—inter-personal relationships, but relationships between potential co-citizens. In other words, I can only be your friend-enemy/enemy-friend if this competition is played out in relation to a specific kind of civic status, that of citizenship. Not only does the friend have to be someone who can be my enemy, they must also be someone who can potentially attain the status of co-citizenship.

My enemy must therefore be someone who can attain the same level of civic meaning as me. You cannot be my enemy and we cannot be in a political relationship, unless we also either share a possible citizenship or are competing over that identity. I can only make war, as a political practice, on those who can be my friend and who can at least be judged according to a certain standard of citizenship. To give an historical example, as a citizen of a democracy, I can only have a truly political relationship, and thus go to war, with those who can potentially be, or in my judgement, have failed to be, because they *should be*, democrats. In a telling moment in *Specters of Marx*, Derrida notes a resonance between Francis Fukuyama's analysis of the end of history and a Christian worldview (Derrida, 1994, p. 60). The recent, at least purported, enthusiasm for spreading democracy partakes of the same logic of mission and conversion that marks the Christian will-to-expansion. In other words, it only requires a slight recalibration to argue that the enthusiasm we proclaim about the universalisation of democracy must also reveal its still animating, but relentlessly undisclosed, religious meaning: I can only make war on you if I believe that you can be and should be not necessarily a Christian, but an historical actor in a world defined by the Christian imaginary: convertibility, uniformity, transparent virtue, achieved revelation and teleological truth. The flip side of this particular logic explains why indigenous peoples in a nation like Australia could be subject to genocidal attack but not one that can even yet be acknowledged as "war." Unable to be mistaken as a friend, or co-citizen, they can never really be enemies, just objects of annihilation, never reaching the threshold of politics.

The entanglement of friendship and enmity culminates in human rights abuse: I torture you, not because you are so other as to terrify me, nor because you are so other that I need to protect myself from your strangeness. I do it because you are potentially my friend, my co-citizen, a democrat or Christian, something you should be, and look you are failing to be it now! In short, this kind of abuse is not a revulsion at otherness, but an enactment of the impossibility of keeping friendship from becoming enmity, the impossibility of attaining to the purity of either friendship or enmity, the impossibility of resolutely separating friendship from enmity in its historical unfolding, the impossibility in short of stopping one from flowing over into the other, of awakening it, or even allowing the two to coincide. We have a fantasy that wars are caused by alienation and the strangeness of the other. Or indeed, we have a fantasy that the other is somehow a stranger to us. The West talks as if it has had no dealing with Islam and does not know it, despite more than a millennium of not only contact, but also intermingling and mutual influence. How could the West possibly believe Islam is a stranger? This strangeness has to be endlessly reinvented as a way of denying a history of intimacy and confusion: we never make war on what is strange to us. The truth is the reverse: we act to make strange what we make war on, disentangling it from what we are and a history of mutual implication.

It would be tempting—and seemingly appropriate—to apply a Levinasian schema here. What would seem to be at stake is the determination on the part of a putative subject to reduce the other to a level of shared identity. You are my enemy because you could be my co-citizen, a democrat or a Christian. But this politics is not to be subjectivised. These markers of identity do not determine the politics here, as much as they are merely its pretext or point of articulation. Even in the deconstruction of Schmitt, the idea of the impersonality of enmity persists. What is at stake is not a determination to annihilate otherness in order to consolidate a self-identical self. What is revealed is the dynamic always latent within any definition of friendship or enmity and thus of politics, the range of possible slippages, confusions and collapses of difference that history can always reveal, events in which I can kill the person I came to protect, I can destroy the village in order to save it, I can be kept free by having my rights taken away from me, and where I can torture in the name of human rights.

What the complexity of the friend/enemy economy stages, therefore, is not a site of subjective truth but a specifically Derridean type of historicity. Derrida discusses how Schmitt's definition of the enemy relies on the "real possibility of war" with them. The real possibility of war is less the announcement of a real event that might or might not happen, as much as a kind of negative messianism: the future event to which we must orient ourselves in order to experience meaning, but whose power resides in the fact that it will not come to pass. This real possibility installs in the heart of Schmitt's argument a kind of suspension that means that the definitions which would seem to rely on this concept become themselves irretrievably unfinished. The distinction between friend and enemy cannot finally be realised, because this real possibility is fundamentally a spectrality. "For what is this 'real possibility' haunting Schmitt if not the very law of *spectrality*?" Derrida writes (Derrida, 1997, p. 129).

Politics is haunted by the real possibility of war. This takes the form of friendship and enmity always lying in wait for one another, threatening one another with that which both defines and ruins each. Friendship can never not be haunted by the possibility of enmity. It cannot be friendship without this possibility latent within it. I can only be your friend because of the possible enmity that I can see within you and that haunts our friendship, and that might at any sudden and eruptive, but always just-with-held, still-future *moment* become you. You are only my friend because you are always about to be my enemy, so that I must be prepared to treat both aspects of you always and at once. Even as I care for you and save you, you threaten me, at least with the threat I must represent to you too, the possibility that we are always already enemies and that

I will hurt you even as I help you. The logic of spectrality can never be reduced to a singularity that will save us from this risk. My concern for you cannot be stopped once and forever from becoming my cruelty towards you. We can fight wars for human rights but there will always be only the thinness of a piece of paper between wars for human rights and wars on human rights. And sometimes not even that.

The deconstruction of the friend/enemy and the war/peace binaries does not free us into a world unpolluted by the authoritarianism of self-identity. The continued assumption that deconstruction is an avenue to a kind of freedom—freedom from the current gender regime, from the centripetal logic of colonialism or from the simplest of racial hierarchies—does not help us here. What the deconstructions that have been the focus of this analysis do is reimmerse us in the historical complexities of our current political situation. They do not offer some beyond of war and peace, for example, but reveal the obscure entanglements too easily and briskly concealed by talk of "war or peace," "war instead of peace" or "peace instead of war." Promoters of war go to war for putative friends—the whole undifferentiated category of "the Iraqi people" for example—who never quite fail to be read as a danger and thus can become the object of torture and massacre. They can be friends, Derrida argues, only if they can also be enemies. The aporia at the heart of the friend/enemy distinction has historical results. On the other hand, to argue that peace can be historically realised—in other words, to argue that it can be not just eschatological—becomes merely a way of pretending that the cessation of hostilities, the withdrawal of troops, for example, can resolve complex economic, diplomatic and strategic inter-relationships, thus leading to a too easy denial of how war is always part of larger continuities that it deflects, but that it did not initiate, and that it often does not complete either. The simple withdrawal of western troops from a certain place does not mean that it is no longer caught up, directly or indirectly, in the economic, environmental and diplomatic campaign the West is always waging under various names. Neither war nor peace protects us from its other.

What is required is an identification of key fault-lines along which political events will develop, not because they supply us with some insight into politics in general, or the general state of global arrangements, but because they help us analyse specific events as they unfold, events that we must deal with on a daily basis. The war/other complex is one such fault-line. Wars are fought on behalf of human rights that themselves unleash atrocities, while they rationalise the dismantling of civic protections half a world away. This complex entanglement is where we live now, a site we must negotiate, and in and about which we must make decisions. Derrida distinguishes the decision, in which there is always some indeterminate factor, from calculation, in which a pre-fixed programme is applied. Decision always involves some confrontation with the unknown, even unknowable, and thus requires some taking on of responsibility. Calculation, on the other hand, is the administration of something already clear, known and beyond question. The subject who applies a pre-fixed programme does not take on any responsibility. In situations in which no simple recourse can be made to the friend/enemy distinction, yet alone to the absolute separation of war from peace, dealing with collective social relationships and their possible violence will always entail a difficult negotiation between alternatives that cannot make themselves resolutely clear, either tactically or ethically. Not to fight might simply mean to withdraw into a moral narcissism where your aggression goes unacknowledged and unspoken, even to yourself, while you continue, perhaps unwittingly, to suck the life-blood from the imbalanced world economy. To fight may mean simply to enact one's cultural inclination to violence as the revelation of truth and apocalypse. In other words, peace might be the most aggressive thing of all and war might be just a form of fiction. To decide about war/peace means making some effort to locate yourself amidst the complex entanglements of political action that can be violence or the withdrawal of violence even at one and the same time. In other words, it requires an address to the particular lineaments of a particular situation in the light of the discourses that have produced the concepts of "war" and "peace" for us.

Schmitt, then, thinks of the political as defined by the figure of the enemy, and "the determined possibility of an actual war" (Derrida, 1997, p. 84). If we now live in a depoliticised age, according to Schmittian logic, it is because we have lost the power to invent the enemy. This enemy is structural, not the object of a personal antipathy or even a collective group hatred. In fact, this enemy has no psychological value at all, because its primary function is to give rise to a political order in thought, not to be the object of any kind of cathexis. Politics requires the enemy, and the end of the enemy is the end not of social conflict, but of the political per se. Similarly, the State requires war; without war, there would be no State. The clash between friend and enemy is not then to be imagined in Schmitt as built on simple difference between identity and otherness. It is a structured, determined opposition, and from the point of view of individual psychology or communal identity could be completely without content.

The enemy then is to be considered a public enemy and gives definition to the public as such, as we have seen. To Schmitt, the enemy must be an "ensemble" (Derrida, 1997, p. 86), a group confronting another group. These groups must always have at least the potential to come into conflict with one another. According to Derrida, Schmitt allows for an easy flow from the possibility of conflict between groups to its eventuality and on to its actuality. To Schmitt, there is apparently no real distinction:

> As soon as war is possible, it is taking place, Schmitt seems to say; presently, in a society of combat, in a community presently at war, since it can present itself to itself, as such, only in reference to this possible war. Whether the war takes place, whether the war is decided upon or declared, is a mere empirical alternative in the face of an essential necessity: war is taking place; it has already begun before it starts, as soon as it is characterised as *eventual* (that is, announced as a non-excluded event in a sort of contingent future). And it is *eventual* as soon as it is *possible*.... As soon as war is possible-eventual, the enemy is present; he is there, his possibility is presently, effectively supposed and structuring. His being-there is effective, he institutes the community as a human community of combat, as a *combating* collectivity.
>
> (Derrida, 1997, p. 86)

War then is the essence of the human group, because it is always implied as the defining form of conflict, and the idea of conflict as the defining logic of human community. The enemy distinction requires wars and rumours of wars as its perpetual horizon. War thus defines the political in a way that nothing else can. It is the end-meaning of conflict. War then need not take place. The material practice of war—war actually taking place—is not necessary, and is merely the side-effect of political meaning, a meaning to which fighting is itself not necessary except as a crude indication of the nature of human relations. These relations only require war as an idea, not as a practice. If the practice happens, this is not the truth or material reality of a hard violence finally arriving, it is merely another, not ever the only, not even the most essential or necessary version of the idea. Actual physical fighting is subordinate to the concept (of the political), not a hard pre-existing material fact that the concept must struggle to abstract.

War is an idea because the enemy is an idea, in service to an idea, politics. Politics would in fact be compromised if hostility were contaminated by anything extraneous to simple friend/enemy logic. War, as we have seen, is compromised if it involves hatred. The other is not to be the object of xenophobia, merely structural opposition. As Derrida paraphrases him, Schmitt insists on ontologising enmity, and seeing combat as "a fundamental anthropology" (Derrida, 1997, p. 123). According to Derrida, this is not to argue that this is an expression of a natural biological drive, nor of personal psychological hostility. "Impossible as it may seem," what we are being asked to think is an anthropological hostility that is "a pure hostility and, ultimately, a purely philosophical one" (p. 124). This hostility understands human life in terms of a possibility that need not be realised, "not the actualisation of a possible but something altogether different: the radicalisation of a possible reality or a real possibility" (p. 124).

What is at stake then is not the reality of which possibility is the announcement or indication. It is the invention of the possibility itself as a reality that counts. Humanity is defined not by what human beings are, but by the possibility that orients them, not the psychological death drive, nor the inborn racial antagonism, but the real structural inevitability.

Real possibility must then be so general that it infiltrates every aspect of social life: "it always demands that the presupposition of real possibility or eventuality be present in a determined mode" (Derrida, 1997, p. 125). The consequence that Derrida draws from this is that war contains more political value the more it is before us as a possibility. The friend/enemy distinction offers us more meaning, the less it is realised. Schmitt's writing does not value real war, therefore, as a definition of the political. Instead, war itself functions only as abstracted. The less war actually happens, the more it functions. The less real the possibility, the more it functions effectively as a real possibility. "[O]ne must conclude that rarefaction intensifies the tension and the revealing power (the 'truth' of the political): the less war there is, the more the hostility, etc."(p. 129). Derrida thus detects "a principle of...spectrality at the heart of this discourse on the political" (p. 130).

War haunts its other, not simply as the memory of past trauma, nor as the dread of future agony, but as the intimidating pressure of an insistent meaning, a specific meaning, one that never leaves "peace," "the social," or "civility" uncompromised. As we have seen, the term "war" is commonly dissociated from actual fighting, even at the State level; on the other hand, the term is also readily applied to developments in the field of social policy and administration—wars on crime, poverty, drugs, obesity and so on. There is nothing simple or straightforward about the use of this word. It is not at all obvious what is or should be considered wars. Nowhere has this been more apparent, or commented on, than in the perhaps bold, probably unwise, possibly absurd, definitely counter-productive declaration of a

War on Terror in 2001. There is a disjunction then between the common meaning of the term "war" and its use. Some other judgement must intervene between the occurrence of armed conflict and its denomination as war. The term itself must have a function separate from the dictionary, or legal, definition. In the concept of "the real possibility of war," as the definition of the political, we see what this function might be. War is not a simple class of human practice, but a way of defining human sociality.

What is important in the Derridean account of the relationship between war and its others is that it argues that the relationship is not one of simple negative determination, where war and whatever we want to contrast with it are alienated from one another in a tense complementarity that sets the limit between them. War infiltrates peace, defining it not by exclusion but because conceptually, there is never a sensible separation between them. Without war, society does not exist, whether it is to be defined in terms of that formation we institute in order to protect ourselves from our nature, or if we see war as the enactment of the hidden essential truth of the social or whether we see war as the transgression social order needs in order to manage the vital pressure towards excess. In "the real possibility of war" as the definition of the political, we see these theories of the social summarised.

Are we to imagine a society without war or avoid the term "society" altogether? Are we to rethink the possibility of social relations outside of the possibility of war or are we to try and work out some way of negotiating the war/other complex, as we have said would be suggested by Derrida's writings on pragmatic politics? The arguments that have presented the relationship between war and its other as a complex entanglement—from psychological ambivalence to deconstructive doubleness—repudiate the idea that a state of Kantian "perpetual peace" is possible where war has been left behind once and for all. It also challenges the inverse idea that the wars we fight are the result of simple enmity, whether that enmity be conceived of as collective hostility, moral polarization or personal antipathy. Neither the pure enmity of alienation nor the pure harmony of reconciliation is ever meaningfully less than fantastic. War and its other can never leave each other alone and must be encountered at all levels of our understanding of what the social might be. On the other hand, antagonism defined as the hostility between others incomprehensible and irreducibly strange to one another must be seen as the attempt to present complex histories of mutual entanglement as moral schema simple enough to license the worst, most cynically naïve and lethal forms of political appropriation.

Part III
The Problem of Difference

Clausewitz's aim in arguing that war was merely an extension of policy had been to bring war into the pragmatic world of political decision-making. More recently, his argument has been restored to a place of prominence and become again the most influential account of the relationship between war and its other. Now, however, the idea that war and civil or political society are in a continuous relationship with one another is intended as a critique of how social relations have been thoroughly compromised by war. It has become a truism that now war has become regularised as both international and domestic policy. The implication is that we need to recover some idea of what is other or opposite to war in order to defeat it. Yet, as we have seen, it is the relationship between war and what is other to it that makes war possible. We will return to this problem in the Conclusion. First let us look at some of the theorists who have analysed war recently, and the emerging consensus that war and its other are losing their difference. We will start by looking at those thinkers who have most strongly insisted on some version of the Clausewitzian view, in which war and its other are seen as somehow continuous with one another.

The collapse of difference: Insisting on Clausewitz

War as the thing that society is formed in order to forestall; war as an activation of a society in its political form: these are models of a war more than intimate with or more than even constitutive of the social. The slightest social fragility, the most meagre political intention may reveal the war bubbling away beneath the placid surface of civil relations. In the Hobbesian account, war emerges wherever the social is under stress, and nature shines through the thin, worn fabric of co-habitation. The sovereign must therefore be protected or strengthened by the greatest trust of its citizenry, who enthusiastically sacrifice their rights, or allow the sovereign sufficient licence, because they know that everywhere the war they fear is under the thinnest social cover, seeking to come back. We learn to distrust our partners in the agreement that established the sovereign because they might lose control of their war-like nature. The sovereign exclusion of war means war is now everywhere in the unfolding of the social, our enduring if alien companion.

In Clausewitz, war emerges easily when society opens its hand. Peace is not ashamed of war and uses it. Policy extends itself into war, drawing the whole of the society with it. The argument is even stronger than this, because policy does not represent the cynical manipulation of the social, seducing or tricking it into war. The impulse of the social is controlled by policy, without which the drive to violence for its own sake, a violence of annihilation of the other, would be even stronger, even wilder.

We have here two very different versions of the social and its relationship with war. Yet both reveal how the alternation of war and the social (war as the social's other, war as the execution of collective social intention) leads to a collapse of the foreign-ness between the two. This foreign-ness is assumed, then elaborately disproved, even if from opposite directions. In Hobbes, society moves away from war, but always drags it with it, as its compelling and unshakeable underside. War accompanies every flexing of the social, every moment, and threatens to overwhelm what is determined to suppress or conceal it. In Clausewitz, society stoops, through policy, to the war that would seem to contradict it, but that is in fact the fullest activation of its energies.

In Michel Foucault's account of the social war, we see something similar, when Foucault cheekily, cleverly, reverses Clausewitz's statement. At the outset of the series of lectures that comprise *Society Must be Defended*, he announces his hypothesis: "[p]ower is war," he writes, "the continuation of war by other means" (Foucault, 2003, p. 15). What this claim implies is that the relations of power in a society do not quell or disable war, but continue it, because they were founded in a real war that really happened and that can be specified. It also means that the establishment of supposedly peaceful social relations by the institution of formal putatively legitimate power is not intended to end or preclude the inequality in relations established in the violent struggle for power. Indeed, the purpose of the establishment of formal power as peace is to reinvigorate war throughout the social, "in institutions, economic inequalities, language, and even the bodies of individuals"

(Foucault, 2003, p. 16). What this means, according to Foucault, is that within all social practices war is continuing in displaced, disguised or re-represented form, undiminished if translated into a wholly other language of articulation. "We are always writing the history of the same war, even when we are writing the history of peace and its institutions" (p. 16).

Foucault sets two ways of analysing power against one another. On the one hand, we have a theory of power in terms of its legitimacy. Sovereignty claims a legal authority, underwritten by a civil contractual logic, in which the natural "primal" (Foucault, 2003, p. 16) right of the individual is surrendered. When this legal authority exceeds itself, the result is tyranny or oppression. On the other hand is another theory of power altogether, one in which the excess of power is not an abuse, but merely the inevitable extension of the logic of dominance that defines social relations, because it is its ancestry. The former is a model of order and hierarchy, where a legally constituted governing power has its limits strictly defined. It may overstep these limits and brutalise, but this violence is always seen as a transgression of its proper power, perhaps one that can be explained in terms of the psychology or incompetence of the historical players periodically entrusted with that power. Beneath the excess, however, the legitimacy of the contract endures, embarrassed by violence and ostensibly separate from it. Violence in the contract system is a mistake. In the alternative model, social power merely translates the divisions and antagonisms of war into another form. Social institutions merely continue the war already well underway—perhaps so long underway, it is rarely recognised as war, even taken for granted. In what Foucault calls here the "war-repression" schema (Foucault, 2003, p. 17), what is at stake is not legitimacy but merely "dominance and submission" (p. 17).

An account of society seen from the point of view of relations of domination, rather than from the evaluation of legitimacy, will reveal a wholly other social logic. Foucault outlines systematically the difference between the two. Foucault claims that European political thought since the Middle Ages has been preoccupied with the issue of the legitimacy of royal power, at the behest of that power. He quotes approvingly Petrarch's complaint "Is there nothing more to history than the praise of Rome?" (Foucault, 2003, p. 74). The sovereign progress of sovereignty as the ostensible clarification and consolidation of the good leads discourse to twin emphases: the legal elaboration of the right of the sovereign and the concomitant explanation of the duties of the subject. In this discourse, the duty to justify legitimacy leads to the assumed obligation to cleanse power of what might seem to compromise it: its reliance on violent domination. Domination is made to disappear and is not seen as intrinsically part of the sovereign power that accompanies it. Foucault produces here an inversion of the relationship between sovereignty and domination. Instead of adopting the more conventional line that dominance is a mere instrument of a sovereign power that pretends to be legitimate but is simply the rationalisation of the centralisation of power in the hands of the few, Foucault locates sovereignty *within* a larger unfolding of dominance. His recent work, he says, has been given over to

> stress the fact of domination in all its brutality and its secrecy, and then to show not only that right is an instrument of that domination...but also how, to what extent, and in what form right...serves as a vehicle for and implements relations that are not relations of sovereignty, but relations of domination.
>
> (Foucault, 2003, p. 27)

It is not that dominance merely serves an established regime by arguing its legitimacy and disguising its violence by formulations of sovereign order. The doctrine of right is merely one aspect of a larger technique of dominance, and is subsequent, subordinate and junior to it. It is this elaborate and widespread mechanics of domination that needs to be revealed. Subordination is not the duty of those subject to legitimate power, but the fate of the dominated, not the acceptance of an authority necessary to save us from ourselves, but the continuation of a brutal violence in which many must forever be kept in check.

The mode of analysis most appropriate to this situation must be unconventional. First, it must look at power not in terms of how its most petty manifestations can be justified from the logic of legitimacy at the putative centre. It must look at power in its most local and peripheral manifestations, at its extremities (Foucault, 2003, p. 27). Secondly, it must not see what is going on at these extremities as explained or reducible to what is intended by sovereignty. To continue to reduce what happens at the periphery to what is intended at the centre ends by obscuring the detailed and particular forms of the operation of power produced as the manner by which we live: "rather than asking ourselves what the sovereign looks like from on high, we should be trying to discover how multiple bodies, forces, energies, matters, desires, thoughts and so on are gradually, progressively, actually and materially constituted as subjects, or as the subject" (p. 28). It is here that Foucault stresses the difference between what he is trying to do and the Hobbesian schema, whereby the particularities of the operation of power in specific local contexts are made sense of by the construction of a single magnificent if monstrous body, where the localisation, plurality, incommensurability and fragmentation of social relations are denied, and where everything is seen as subordinate to a single logic of necessary legitimacy, a legitimacy to which all local grievances and desires are to be subject. As we have seen, this legitimacy is partly justified by its claim to be the only way in which our desires can in fact be satisfied. If we were left to our desires, our desires would not be fulfilled. Only by denying our desire can we have it. If, as in Foucault's view, the Leviathan is the "central soul" (p. 29) which obscures the detailed operation of power in its peripheral effects, then its complex logic of desire can be explained in another way: the desire of the individual subject is always and forever wrong, an illegitimate desire to be measured against the desire legitimated by the imagined social centre. The Leviathan thus produces an apparently "natural" desire whose function is to be contradicted by the correct desire sovereignty makes acceptable. Following the logic of Foucault's argument, therefore, sovereignty's imagined centralisation is really just itself something that operates to pressure what happens at the peripheral and local. The centre is just an image deployed at the periphery. The choice of terms like "centre" and "periphery" therefore is merely a way of disputing a political fiction on its own terms, not a reversal of priorities. Foucault is not arguing that we must suppress the centre and pay attention to the under-privileged periphery: there is only a periphery, where the centre functions merely as an image of an absent and unreachable ideal, one whose only function is to influence what happens locally. This is because power operates in endlessly mobile and fluid networks, where individual localities are constantly reinventing their relationship with one another, not as regions of a hierarchical system that makes sense from the top down. The local both operates and receives these flows of power.

In sum, then, Foucault sees political analysis that concentrates on the issue of legitimacy imagined by Hobbes as the Leviathan as overlooking the more compelling and pragmatic issue of the techniques of the operation of dominance within which we live. Sovereignty is a seductive issue, a "trap" (Foucault, 2003, p. 34). Each side of the social struggle has used sovereignty for its own purposes, ignoring the new modality of power that has risen alongside sovereignty, producing its own prolix discourses, not of the legitimacy of sovereign right, but of the standards of normalising truth. This new style of power that Foucault calls "disciplinary power" (p. 36) is "absolutely incompatible" (p. 35) with sovereignty. Yet, it is between these two styles of power that since the nineteenth century, modern political life has unfolded in a tortuous negotiation between overt and tactical discourses of right and half-concealed but insistent routines of discipline. The two cannot be reduced to one another and are radically disjunctive but they "necessarily go together" (p. 37).

The saturation of the social body by petty relations of domination reveals a political organisation whose tendency is not towards the clarification and refinement of right, but towards an endless struggle. This struggle, Foucault argues, lies behind the structures of law. Law, he says, was "not born of nature...but of real battles, victories, massacres and conquests" (p. 50). These wars are not abstract or hypothetical. They can be precisely identified. He writes,

> Law is not pacification, for beneath the law, war continues to rage in all the mechanisms of power, even in the most regular. War is the motor behind institutions and order. In the smallest of its cogs, peace is waging a secret war...we have to interpret the war that is going on beneath peace; peace itself is a coded war. We are therefore at war with one another; a battlefront runs through the whole of society, continuously and permanently, and it is this battlefront that puts us all on one side or the other. There is no such thing as a neutral subject. We are all inevitably someone's adversary.
> (Foucault, pp. 50–1)

This perpetual struggle, which will be decided not by an adjudication of right, but by someone's victory and someone else's defeat, is immanent to all social relations. The discourse of sovereignty, which has done so much to distract us from this unfolding struggle, is merely a tactic in this battle, producing seductive and mystifying discourses of law and right. Beneath the condescension of universalising right, struggle goes on without let-up, the real struggle, the social war, the persistence of a war, explained away or supposedly overcome by right.

Foucault's own writing then sees itself as both commemorating and activating an alternative concealed tradition of historico-political writing, the first legitimate one, he claims, since medieval times (Foucault, 2003, p. 52). This legitimacy derives from the discourse's awareness that it is itself taking sides and is a weapon in a struggle. The discourse of sovereignty denies its implication in, even subordination to, this struggle, setting up the chimera of legitimacy as worse than a ruse. The discourse of struggle has its own logic of right, but not of a universal transcendental right, or particular and partisan rights, once owned, then lost, now to be recovered. This discourse is unashamedly "perpectival" (p. 52).

When it gives a complete account of the social struggle, arguing its own truth, presenting its own map of others' positions and motives, it does so tendentiously, using the truth as a weapon in its own campaigns, resisting the claim to universal, eternal and impersonal truthfulness. Truth as a tactic, then, not as an identity. The "pacified universality" (p. 53) of juridico-political discourse ascendant since Ancient Greece is challenged, under threat. This discourse does not descend from the abstract and totalising domain of the super-human metaphysical. It rises from the below of society (p. 54), from the chaos, confusion and dim perceptions that are all available within the bitter and desperate grounds of the struggle itself. The partisanship is on the ground of the fight. It is deflected into dim disproportions, refracted by particular angularities. It is in and of the struggle, it is the struggle itself. It is praised and activated by Foucault, even in its dark and poisonous hatred, and in its cruel and desperate luxury, he half-identifies his own hard discourse with it. We see here the cool historian–jurist–philosopher revealing what lies behind his own tropes of violence and war, of deployments, tactics, of occupation and regimen. The sound of politics may seem to be vociferous debate, but that is merely misheard gunfire. It is that double sound with which Foucault wants to compare his own writing. This writing of history as struggle must remain bitter. It cannot be allowed to make sense. The risk of dialectical thinking as an alternative model of social struggle is that it ends by subordinating itself to a logic of order, resolution and identification, the redemption of the cruelty of struggle in the piety of sensible progress (Foucault, 2003, p. 58).

What is the nature of the struggle that lies behind the placid anaemic smile of the social face? From the seventeenth century on, it has become increasingly clear that "the war that is going on beneath order and peace, the war that undermines our society and divides it in a binary mode is, basically, a race war" (Foucault, 2003, pp. 59–60). Social division is recast not around the science of political structures, nor the investment of class prerogatives, but around the bitterness of an inherited fight to the end. Society is divided into two imagined groups at loggerheads with one another, and the way these groups present themselves is constantly transforming itself, from the crystallisation of ancient grievances through notionally tribal localism to modern scientific racism. Yet what endures beneath is a struggle where there is only partisanship, and universalism is either a tactic or a distraction. At the end of the Middle Ages, in the sixteenth and seventeenth centuries, history ceases to laud and advance sovereignty and becomes "a discourse about races, about a confrontation between races, about the race struggle that goes on within nations and within laws" (Foucault, 2003, p. 69). Hence, the scepticism that develops in historical discourse, according to Foucault, where the behaviour of kings and the powerful appear as deceptive, where the discourse of power is distrusted, and where history itself is to be seen as probably always partisan. Historical discourse becomes an unsettled relationship between the definition and defence of sovereignty, on the one hand, and the insinuations of the race war, on the other. Yet, these two histories can easily become confused, so the denials each must make in order for it to be understood what it is for are never completely to be believed. Partisan history articulates its own view of the whole; sovereign history is seen as a tool of the powerful.

In the first half of the nineteenth century, the race struggle undergoes a bifurcation and a modernisation. Now two historical discourses counter to the logic of sovereignty emerge: on one hand, a counter-history which reads the race struggle as a class war and, on the other hand, the race struggle which morphs into modern racism, by adopting the logic of the burgeoning sciences of biology and medicine, and letting the contingency of historical meaning fade into the necessity of biological essence:

> This racism takes over and reconverts the form and function of the discourse on race struggle, but it distorts them, and it will be characterised by the fact that the theme of historical war—with its battles, its invasions, its looting, its victories, and its defeats—will be replaced by the postevolutionist theme of the struggle for existence.
> (Foucault, 2003, p. 80)

To Foucault, this is the point at which modern racism begins: "when the theme of racial purity replaces that of race struggle, and when counter-history begins to be converted into a biological racism" (p. 81).

The destination of this particular way of thinking about society is to transform your antagonist into, not the rival in an internecine struggle, but *the threat within*. The race struggle becomes then not the competition between two social fractions for dominance, but the invention of an insidious, even cancerous alien presence, arising and threatening from within:

> We see the emergence of the idea of an internal war that defends society against threats born of and in its own body. The idea of social war makes...a great retreat from the historical to the biological, from the constituent to the medical.
> (Foucault, 2003, p. 216)

The Problem of Difference 127

The rival for dominance becomes the contaminating other. This other is transformed from competitor for power to biological toxin. So intense is the threat that this other proposes, it perhaps has to be represented as dominant, as an instituted injustice, where the undeserving, perhaps even despite all evidence, are seen to exercise, insidiously, perhaps invisibly, some secret, magical control. The race war transforms itself from an argument about competing grievances to a campaign of self-cleansing, from struggle to therapy, from violence to hygiene. A clash of powers becomes a drive for self-purification. Ethnicity becomes an issue and it must be cleansed. Genocide becomes visible as the spawn of science. A new State-defined universality, of the national destiny, the norm and the pure race becomes sanctioned (Foucault, 2003, p. 225).

Sovereignty and the disciplinary society give way then to a new emphasis, where the population becomes the focus of administration. Where the theory of right understood society as built around a range of contractual relationships regularised into hierarchies, and the disciplinary society focussed on the management of the individual, the society of bio-power addresses human beings as a collective biological problem:

> What we are dealing with in this new technology of power is not exactly society (or at least not the social body, as defined by the jurists). Nor is it the individual-as-body. It is a new body, a multiple body, a body with so many heads that, while they might not be infinite in number, cannot necessarily be counted. Biopolitics deals with the population, with the population as political problem, as a problem that is at once scientific and political, as a biological problem and as power's problem.
>
> (Foucault, 2003, p. 245)

The rise of the disciplinary society then as the animation of society as a site of power, of dominance and subordination, reveals and allows to arise the war over the bare life, as Agamben will call it, of biologically defined groups. Discipline is intensified as biopolitics, revealing the necessarily collective lineaments of the race struggle.

The disciplinary society focuses on the individual by applying the norm; biopolitics turns the logic of collective identity that the norm articulates into a map of the population reduced from an active political plurality with putative agency into a problem of macro-social planning. The enemy race becomes then a problem of historical management, not a rival with equal subjectivity to be defeated and dominated, nor a deviation to be regularised, but a threat to be exterminated. The State then is justified in applying its unrivalled social power—the monopoly on physical force that it has legislated—to defend the "population" (Foucault, 2003, p. 256), if necessary by the most unsparing generalisation and rationalisation of collective murder.

Racism and war then are identified with one another in Foucault's account. A mythical history has been invented through the course of Europe's second millennium, in which an ancient war is deemed unresolved, producing two rival races, one ostensibly dominant and exercising rights it has no just claim to; the second, embittered because it has lost its rights, agitates endlessly for its claims to be honoured. It sees law as not the progressive establishment of a rational and universal order, but the tool used cynically by the powerful unentitled. It sees sovereignty not as the guarantee of a meaningful if authoritarian order, but the mask behind which hides an illegitimate rule, a rule by thieves. Foucault endorses this reading of a society conforming to a logic of dominance and subordination. The saturation of society by power re-makes not only every relationship, but every identity, and even—even most of all—individual subjectivity becomes a creature and vehicle of that power. A society in which power is present and active in even the pettiest, most hidden locus becomes regulated around norms that become increasingly medicalised. Irregularity becomes pathological, but not simply at the level of the individual, in the formation of a legitimate population, that draws its legitimacy from its long anger over its dispossession. It is legitimate but still also dispossessed, unjustly dominated by a secret cabal, a foreigner, a usurping race, manipulator of a secret system of control, an international banking network, a capitalist-Bolshevik-Jewish one for example, but hidden, so hidden, so secretive there is no evidence for it, and what could be more damning than that? What could prove more clearly the insidiousness of the evil usurping race than how completely it has erased the traces of its dominance? Invisible, calculating, poisonous: the enemy of legitimacy becomes the enemy of life. The usurping race becomes biological infestation. The war over legitimacy has become a war over life in which not only the infesting life must be rooted out, but one's proper life must be strengthened: there is an uneven and interrupted but persistent continuity that runs from the war of lost rights, to the war of ruthless purity. Foucault writes,

> War. How can one not only wage war on one's adversaries but also expose one's own citizens to war, and let them be killed by the million...except by activating the theme of racism? From this point onward, war is about two things: it is not simply a matter of

destroying a political adversary, but of destroying the enemy race, of destroying that [sort] of biological threat that those people over there represent to our race. In one sense, of course, this is no more than a biological extrapolation from the theme of the political enemy. But there is more to it than that. In the nineteenth century—and this is completely new—war will be seen as a way of not only improving one's race by eliminating the enemy race (in accordance with the themes of natural selection and the struggle for existence), but also as a way of regenerating one's own race. As more and more of our number die, the race to which we belong will become purer.

(Foucault, 2003, p. 257)

In Clausewitz, the political class controlled the native energy of the people, activating and directing this innate violence towards some purpose. War is the whole society made fatal. Foucault shares this conclusion, but Clausewitz's argument demonstrates his point: a sovereignty manipulating the dominated so that their violence can be turned against some outsider, for what they must be deceived to believe is their own purpose. In Foucault, this would not be a rationalisation of social warfare, but an example of the weird ways in which it can unfold. Yet, both see war as the maximum activation of the logic of the social, turned both outwards (towards the diplomatic foe, in one account, the enemy race in the other) and inwards (to control unstable social energy; the enemy is in fact concealed within). Society makes itself in its wars.

In Hobbes and Kant, we only attain society through war. We must overcome war in order to reach the social pact that sovereignty represents. War, then, is traceable at every point in the social fabric, largely taking the form of repudiation of war and the fear of constantly slipping back into it. In Clausewitz, on the other hand, war is the activation of the social, the means by which the society unleashes its energy and directs it towards rational goals. In Foucault, the social, war's reputed other, merely becomes the means by which the hidden war plays out its relations of domination and subordination. War and the social are co-ordinated, and the latter's ostensible repudiation of war—its insistence on law, sovereignty, order and peace—are merely instruments and images further manipulated as weapons in the social war. The tension between war and its other is merely illusory here. This understanding of society as perpetual agony has of course been highly influential and adept at understanding the brutal nature of social administration. As the epitome of his work, which has proven so rich and influential a contribution to our understanding of modern social organisation, Foucault's account of war here is confronting and insightful. It is curiously unproblematic, however. Foucault's work attracts us because it allows us to see the raw brutality of power at work in the clinical diagnosis, the legal judgement, the social policy, and even the queue at a government agency. His account of war is part of a horrific model of the social. His view of war is provocative but, curiously, not especially difficult, because it sidesteps the issue raised by the strand of theory we have traced from Freud to Derrida: the one that wants to see not just the co-ordination between war and its other, but how that coordination coincides with the clash between them, a clash that we cannot ignore if we are to understand the complexity of a world in which we still fight in order to secure peace, imprison and torture in the name of freedom, and bomb to advance human rights.

The most complete version of the idea that there is a convergence between war and civil society is in Paul Virilio's extended account of the historico-social development that leads to the domination of post-modern society by logistics, and the reduction of the political to near redundancy in societies dominated by technologies of increasing speed. In *Speed and Politics* (1977), Virilio traces these developments from the foundation of the bourgeois city to the global dominance of Mutually Assured Destruction, in the Cold War period. Virilio sees this transition as achieving what Clausewitz had fore-warned. Clausewitz, Virilio argues, had seen the political class as some brake on the full disclosure of the violence of society, what we have already seen in terms of war as the total activation of the social. The demotion of the political class is the result of the increasing speed of technology—arriving at near instantaneousness in the period dominated by the threat of global nuclear war—which reduces the scope for consideration and decision to near zero. The marginalisation of politics is the culmination of the process whereby the logic of warfare colonises the social. Where in Clausewitz, the "full discharge" (Virilio, 1986, p. 129) of war was the result of the unleashing of violence natural to the mass of humanity, in Virilio it is made possible by the complete saturation of the social with military logic, what he calls "pure war" (Virilio and Lotringer). In short, for Virilio, the advance of technology has not only reduced the ability of war's other to check and challenge it, but has transformed it—specifically the social order of political decision-making—into something war-like. In the form of the logistical, what is other to war takes on war-dress. The difference between war and its other disappears.

The development of this process is traced from the rise of the city as itself a point on a vector, rather than an established centre, which all else serves. Virilio argues that cities should not be understood as fixed and established institutions to which channels of communication are subordinate. Roads are not merely the ways in which cities join up with one another. Cities, in fact, are interruptions of processes of transit made habitable. They are defined not by their stable identity, their economic function nor their communal solidarity. They are points defined by the vectors of transit they punctuate. Their function is as much strategic as democratic. They pioneered the idea of local organisations as first and foremost strategic. In the city, concentrations of population become organised as fortresses. This is the start of a process whereby the whole of society, initially in its physical dispersal, becomes totalised as a military formation. Virilio writes,

> The political triumph of the bourgeois revolution consists in spreading the state of siege of the communal city-machine, immobile in the middle of its logistic glacis and domestic lodgings, over the totality of the national territory.
>
> (Virilio, 1986, p. 14)

Virilio pays particular attention to the ways in which the wars of the twentieth century have contributed to this process. The "war of attrition" in the First World War signalled that the working classes had become a kind of military proletariat, less important either as a cog in the economic machine or even as potentially heroic and individualised warriors, but those who transform the environment into a radically militarised one. This transformation of space from resource landscape to site of interminable struggle also marked the transition from wars over space to wars imagined in terms of time. Virilio writes,

> The war of attrition had, from lack of space, spread out into Time, duration was survival. All terrain (or rather, sans-terrain) assault extends war over an earth that disappears, crushed under the infinity of possible trajectories.
>
> (Virilio, 1986, p. 56)

As war could not be measured in terms of domination of territory, what counted was the ability to sustain struggle indefinitely in a space defined as a purely potential site of war. The earth itself becomes graphically militarised. The construction of infrastructure by the militarised proletariat gives the countryside over to a new state as the site of the perpetual anticipation—or non-deferment—of inevitable warfare. War becomes ubiquitous in "the creation of the original infrastructure of future battlefields" (Virilio, 1986, p. 53). The human relationship with the earth is radically remade by this projection of war into time. War is defined not in terms of the conquest of space, but the preparation of space for the site of a future struggle, one virtually immanent, not militarily dramatic. War "is not exercised against a more or less determined military adversary, but as a permanent assault on the world" (p. 64).

This transformation of the relationship with the earth is part of the subordination of human values to the impetus of technology and the cardinal factor in this process is the speed of weapons systems. The latter, in fact, drives history, according to Virilio (p. 68). Individuals no longer operate as embodiments of civic identity, but become, in the phrase used so effectively by Deleuze and Guattari, each and every one, a "war-machine" (p. 90). The proletarian worker whose aim is merely to support the development of war-infrastructure, on the one hand, and, on the other, the proletarian soldier rushing into battle become indistinguishable. The opening up of the landscape to the preparation for war leads inevitably to the erasure of difference between war and civil society:

> These first attempts at penetration, clandestine "invasion" of the social corpus, had, as we saw, a specific aim: exploitation by the armed forces of the nation's raw potential (its industrial, economic, demographic, cultural, scientific, political and moral capabilities). Since then, social penetration has been linked to the dizzying evolution of military penetration techniques; each vehicular advance erases a distinction between the army and civilisation.
> (Virilio, 1986, p. 106)

Knowingly or unknowingly, as the whole of society assumes the burdens, transitions, the planning and aggression of logistical thinking, the whole society becomes co-ordinated with the military, a collective latent war-machine. The cult of speed penetrates modern consumerism as effectively as it does the teleologies of industry and warfare. We all become "unknown soldiers of the order of speeds" (p. 119). Virilio famously drew a parallel between the development of modern warfare and cinema. This is a cardinal example of the subordination of civilian culture to not just the politics, but the style of war. The history of cinema is entangled in the history of warfare, following a shared path of technological evolution: the role of film in the history of aerial warfare as a method of recording the complexities of high-speed combat and the success or failure of mass bombing being the clearest example. Cinema, however, also takes on a logistical organisation, according to Virilio: the great auteur directors are themselves kinds of dictators or generals at least. "War is cinema, and cinema is war," he writes (Virilio, 1989, p. 26).

The rise of speed as the determining value in warfare means the collapse of the importance of geographic extension as the meaning of strategic advantage. The world itself is defeated (Virilio, 1986, p. 133), resulting in the "geostrategic homogenisation of the globe" (p. 135). The planet itself becomes subordinated to the virtuality of war, no longer a site of progressive development, nor even its negative, political expansion. The earth is miniaturised, "diminished" (p. 135), to the point that distance becomes meaningless, and we live in a situation defined by "the direct encounter of every surface on the globe…the juxtaposition of every locality, all matter" (p. 136). Warfare itself is no longer fought over territory. "The countdown becomes the scene of battle, the final frontier" (p. 138). War becomes reduced to the decision to deploy weapons. The decision becomes subject to the speed of deployment that the weapon itself makes possible. Because the decision to fire sets in motion technical procedures that are as rapid as they are irreversible, the decision itself—accelerated to the point of a kind of automaticity to which political evaluation is unavailable—becomes the war. In fact, since the decision is a mere space in the inevitable operation of the technology, the impetus of the machine itself dictates war to us. The "war-machine suddenly becomes (thanks to the reflexes of the strategic calculator) the very decision for war" (Virilio, 1986, pp. 139–40).

Virilio's analysis is totally—and only—at home in a world where war means shared nuclear annihilation. He states in *Pure War* that "war today is either nuclear war or nothing" (Virilio and Lotringer, 1983, p. 26). He could not see that the war of insurgency, so recently so successful in Vietnam, and about to be so successful against the Soviet Union in Afghanistan (in a struggle that would in fact end the Cold War he wanted to see as the fulfilment of western technological and urban history), would endure, indeed triumph as the model of effective late modern war. Regardless of the fact that Virilio's analysis has been, at least temporarily, marginalised by history, it is worth looking further at what he means by the triumph of logistics, because regardless of the stature of nuclear war in defining contemporary warfare, the influence of logistics on modern society persists. The trace of nuclear emergency endures as the now ubiquitous logic which understands social being in terms of calculation and audit, regardless of the fact that the marginalisation of nuclear war means this way of thinking may have lost its parent.

As we have seen, one of the cardinal events in the development of war through the twentieth century, according to Virilio, is the gearing of the supposedly civilian economy to warfare. This development results in a redefinition of the world itself—and eventually the whole globe—as the mere setting for possible wars. War becomes virtual, subject to the logic of collective planning. It is this development that gives birth to a specific way of thinking in which the whole of the civilian economy becomes the servant of a larger, less patient method. This logic is *logistics*:

> The trucks bringing ammunition and the flying shells bringing death are coupled in a system of vectors, of production, transportation, execution. There we have a whole flow-chart which is logistics itself. To understand what this a-national logistical revolution—Eisenhower's—is, there's a statement by the Pentagon from around 1945–50 which is extraordinary: "Logistics is the procedure following which a nation's potential is transferred to its armed forces, in times of peace as in times of war."
> (Virilio and Lotringer, 1983, p. 16)

This transformation results in us all becoming "civilian soldiers without knowing it" (Virilio and Lotringer, 1983, p. 18). Through logistics, war is important not as international violence or the harbinger of civil chaos but as the invisible essence of planning, teleological thinking and calculation that is the essence or philosophy of technology that in the guise of technology infiltrates every aspect of society:

> That's what the military class is, that kind of unbridled intelligence which gets its absence of limits from technology, from science. The war-machine is not only explosives, it's also communications, vectorization. It's essentially the speed of delivery. When Esso tells the French national train company we'll stop delivering containers, materials, gasoline, oil, refining products, unless you guarantee us trains with 4000-ton capacity running at an average of 100 km/hr; when Esso threatens to make do with trucks, it's already war. Pure war, not the kind which is declared.
> (Virilio and Lotringer, 1983, p. 20)

The domination of all social planning by speed is the result of the acceleration of military technology. Lotringer says to Virilio: "So the primacy of speed is simultaneously the primacy of the military," to which Virilio replies: "Absolutely...what is at the centre is no longer a monarch by divine right, an absolute monarch, but an *absolute weapon*. The center is no longer occupied by a political power, but by a capacity for absolute destruction" (Virilio and Lotringer, 1983, p. 46). The most important thing about this weapon is not its material destructiveness, but the havoc that it has wreaked on social relations. There has been a process of what Virilio calls "endo-colonization" (p. 54), where the war that is supposed to define the frontiers of inter-social tension destroys the culture and structures of peace within the societies it is nominally supposed to protect. Logistics works not by making certain types of warfare possible. Its danger is not that it facilitates violence but that it puts every aspect of social being on a war-footing, invisibly transforming all social interactions into virtually militarised ones. War wins regardless of whether it is fought or not, because it has taken ownership of society, even just in the form of the logistical means and ends thinking that warfare has bequeathed to the world. After nearly a generation since business school graduates started reading Sun Tzu, post-modern corporations and even public institutions now operate according to a rhetoric of strategies and tactics, deployments and fall-back positions, winners and losers, of ramping-up and standing-down. This, to Virilio, is the triumph of technological thinking: "the triumph of technology is Pure War" (Virilio and Lotringer, 1983, p. 54). Logistics no longer simply operates in service of war, but has become the meaning of war. In the age of the nuclear weapon, merely having weapon systems available and being ready to deploy them, in other words, having logistical superiority is already a kind of victory.

The saturation of society by logistical thinking, war not as fighting, but as "infinite preparation" (p. 92), Pure War or the endo-colonisation of the social by war stunts the development of the social. Political ideology gives way to the tyranny of planning and order (p. 96). The whole social machine has to be *geared* from the top down. Endo-colonisation not only results in a sort of techno-organisation of the social, but also in a concomitant change in the way in which time is experienced. Extensive time, the time of historical thinking and political deliberation, is replaced by an emphasis on the intensity of time, the time of "the state of emergency...where what counts is the quality of the instant...it will no longer be important to last but to 'get a thrill'—the quality of life will depend on the intensity of the instant, and not the stability of duration" (pp. 98–9).

In Virilio, then, the logistical subordinates the social to a culture where speed dominates, in the form of means and ends thinking, infinite preparation for war and the intensity of experience, at the expense of the deliberate unfolding of historical time. The result is a culture of impatience for technological goals rather than the fulfilment of chosen meaning, of a haphazard and impulsive calculation, rather than considered reflection deciding on the good and the true. Part insightful critique, part fanciful nostalgia, it is no surprise that Virilio has been criticised as simply indiscriminately techno-phobic (see Kellner, 2000).

In *The Information Bomb* (1998), this indictment of technology reaches new heights. Here, Virilio argues that contemporary science has fallen victim to a constant drive towards the limit, a kind of adventurism that has abandoned human need and logic in a "post-scientific extremism" (Virilio, 2000, p. 2). This drive has made available technological resources disconnected from human decision-making in the economic sphere as MAD had done in the military. Now, global, especially US, corporations have the potential to overrule the decision-making processes of sovereign nation states. "The information bomb has taken over from the atom bomb and is capable of using the interactivity of information to wreck the peace between nations" (Virilio, 2000, p. 63). If the speed of decision-making in the Cold War reduced political decision-making within the state to a degree zero, then the uncontrolled flow of information draws all nations into a global capitalist network where national governments play a negligible role in regulating the activities that traverse their territories. This is a new kind of logistics, a new way in which social logic is saturated with a military style of thinking: "what we see here is the launch of a new logistics, that of the cybernetic control of knowledge: politico-economic knowledge in which the single market affords a glimpse of its military and strategic dimension in terms of 'information transfer'" (Virilio, 2000, p. 133). The United States has declared "electro-economic war" (p. 134) on the world, robbing nations of any hope of political autonomy, enacting a new era of colonisation, in which "cyber-glaciation" supplants "nuclear deterrence" (p. 134).

This information warfare threatens the complete elimination of all kinds of political autonomy, from individualism to the autonomy of the political state. Beneath this lies the amoral adventurism of the new techno-excess, the post-scientific radicalism of science in its endless ambition and adventurism. Virilio concludes,

> We can see now that, just as the total war outlined at the end of the First World War was to be actualised during the Second, threatening, between 1939 and 1945, with Hiroshima and Auschwitz, not the enemy but the human race, the **global warfare** prefigured today in the great manoeuvres of "information warfare" will be based on a scientific radicalisation, threatening—not so much with extermination as with extinction—not a particular population or even the human race

(as the thermo-nuclear bomb might), but the very principle of all individuated life, the *genetic and information* bombs now forming a single "weapons system."

(Virilio, 2000, p. 140)

The apocalyptic view here is a vision of historical risk as undifferentiated. In the same way that Virilio's understanding of the Cold War presented a view of the future where everything would be smashed in a single event, he imagines here how information will consume us all equally and in the same way. Here, differentiation appears not as the disproportion and disconnection between different, even if concurrent, zones of historical experience—to Virilio, there is only one world and one sequence of events. Instead, differentiation is only ever the means by which a single regime divides us from one another in its administration of a single world system. Yet, the universality of the Cold War has given way to a world of conflict, fought out by gangs and governments, sometimes mistakable for one another, with different goals, methods and claims. This is the world Herfried Münkler describes in *The New Wars* (2005). Indeed, such a world always accompanied the Cold War. Mostly, this was all the Cold War ever really was. The different agendas of dominant states, failed state and state-fractions, gangs, organised crime, terrorist organisations, para-military groups, and all the coalitions between them reveal that each and every war is contradicted by the other wars that seek to reverse it, quell it, subsume it or snuff it out altogether. These counter-wars are commonly in the service of what we have called here war's other: sovereignty, law, peace or various civil values. In short, the universalism of Virilio's view suppresses the necessary challenge to war at the heart of every war itself.

The other problem with Virilio's account is in the opposite direction, to do not with the erasure of difference but the dream of recovering it. Virilio is an important link in the chain of thought that sees war and civil society as largely in-different to one another. It is in that sense in a similar vein to the arguments we have seen in Clausewitz and Foucault, but with one significant difference. In Clausewitz and Foucault, war and peace are mere disguises for one another. War is *really* society enacting itself or society is *really* war continued. In Virilio, war is defeating society, colonising it. Virilio keeps alive the sense of war and peace as conceptually different to one another. There really is war, on the one hand, and peaceful civil society, on the other. They are not simply versions of one another. What we see here is a logic of cataclysm, framed by a memory of what has been lost, and, thus, hypothetically at least, a dream of redemption. Here, civil society has been overtaken by war, not because of some essential homology between them, but as a disastrous historical event. By his faith in this difference, Virilio hopes for a possible recovery of the political deliberation logistics and technology have erased. Yet, this opposition is too simple. The ability of logistics to endo-colonise peace must reveal at least some potential similarity and correspondence between the arts of war and the ways of peace. Virilio's argument must rely on this assumption. In other words, the implied radical separation is irrecoverable because of the irreducible commonality. The contrast and the commonality work together. It is this problematic that the theorists of the war/other complex in Part II have attempted to theorise. Virilio reveals such complexity but attempts an account that does not acknowledge it.

As we have seen, the Clausewitzian understanding of the relationship between war and politics is enduringly influential. Foucault and Virilio are its most important recent adherents, though its use is widespread. It is often seen as a reference point without being scrutinised adequately. It appeals to the realist in all of us, those social critics who want to see war as the ruthless calculation of the cynical, on the one hand, and, on the other, those who want to see it as the inevitable resort of those undeluded pragmatists who should be entrusted with world-management. In other words, it is a highly seductive account of war, and difficult to resist if war is to be used as a lens through which to scrutinise politics. Yet, as we have seen, Clausewitz's account is a specific and tightly structured one: in its complete form, it argues not only that war should be understood as an instrument of politics, but also something far more complicated: if war is to fulfil its proper vocation as the tool of policy, it does so in the act of the military genius controlling the tendency of the people towards total war. The people, driven not by rational purpose but by the wild interest of their partisanship, need to have the violent energy of their antagonism directed, so that ideal war, a war for nothing but its own sake, does not overwhelm the purposefulness of policy. This is a more nuanced account than is usually recognised. It does endorse the view of modern war as one in which the different parts of the nation can act in a co-ordinated fashion to pursue collective goals. However, it does recognise the instability of this war formation: there is a tension between policy and tendency. This is what makes the figure of the genius indispensable. Only the mysterious talent of the genius can bring rational calculation and violent energy together.

In the vulgar Clausewitzian doxa that continually resurfaces in accounts of war, this tension is overlooked. Instead, we simply get the lumpen idea that war is merely the collectivity in action in pursuit of its ambitions. There are several problems with this account. First, it does not recognise the fluidity of Clausewitz's model of the group: what he was describing was how, in war, the nation comes into being as the co-ordination between politics and the people. War is not the expression of a social form here, but its enactment, indeed its formation. Secondly, it usually avoids the theoretical problem of the theorisation of the group as a social agent, which alone would allow such accounts to make sense: what is the intention or even purpose of a nation? Where does it reside? In the politicians, who govern, and then who are they, and how does collective intention arise from the machinations of their chamber politics? How does their specific and located intention come to represent that of the group? Or do we merely intuit collective intention retrospectively, assuming that what a group does must be a symptom of what they—consciously or unconsciously—intended? Therefore, if a nation expands, then expansion must have been its mission. Such accounts inevitably end by collapsing their understanding of the social into war itself. The relationship between war and the social becomes chiasmatic, even tautological. War is the act of the social. In turn, the social becomes merely that which acts in war. The social is reduced to that which puts war into effect. This is not necessarily presented as a positive model of society, but rather slips into analysis as the default position to which social relations are inevitably reduced. The consequences of this, as we will see, is that concession is too easily made to the realist account of international relations, which quickly becomes a kind of inverted naivety, an acceptance of a kind of hard balance of global power as somehow the best we can hope for.

I will take Paul Hirst's account of space in warfare: *Space and Power: Politics, War and Architecture* (2005) as an illustration of this problem in contemporary thinking. Hirst accepts Clausewitz's description of war uncritically (Hirst, 2005, p. 53), as if there are no serious alternatives. "War is the organised pursuit of interest by means of force," he writes (p. 51). This simple formulation is used to read a vast array of different historical events across Western history, including the invasion of the Americas and the conflicts between Christian and Islamic forces both within and on Europe's borders. I would like to take one brief example. In a discussion of the Reconquest of Spain, Hirst writes,

> In the decisive phases of the Reconquest, local frontier-fighting was central and it promoted both social mobility and freedom. Servile obligations were inconsistent with life on the frontier and the

necessity of military service for as many males as possible...The frontier drew enterprising spirits from the interior. In an underpopulated land, it forced the Crown and major lords to maintain rights and incentives further back in the chain to keep people from the lure of the frontier. For the minor aristocracy and the commoner knights, war and raiding provided opportunities that were not equalled by normal economic activity: thus the advancing frontier fed on itself.

(Hirst, 2005, p. 84)

Here, war and the social are one co-ordinated social machine, in which the needs of expansion and the evolution of social relations are parts of a single process. Agency is given to impersonal phenomena. It is the frontier and frontier-fighting which govern social change, and that indeed take all the initiative here. The activity of human agents is not put into effect in frontier-fighting, but becomes decisive only as part of what fighting unfolds. The movement of the frontier becomes an almost automatic and reflexive human activity, but it is not clear how it became policy or whether it can even be considered as policy. A traditional conception of the human as always expanding, and only able to satisfy its economic and ideological wants by expansion, is taken as read, at both an individual and a collective level. Intention then is not a preconceived and determined plan that then finds its means in warfare. Warfare is the only access to otherwise undisclosed intentions, which then become identified with what warfare might seem to be able to achieve. War becomes not an instrument of social policy, but becomes that policy. It becomes what the society is doing, and thus it must be seen to reveal its purpose, even if that purpose is not formulated. Society becomes the residence of some imaginary or intuited purpose, one only made real in war. As a result, society is merely the back-formation from war. It is that which enacts itself in and through war. In this context, Hirst's claim that a society like Castile was "a military society" (Hirst, 2005, p. 83) geared to the practical pursuit of interest becomes incontestable. Throughout *Space and Power*, the interest of the social group is always everywhere seen as revealed in the strategic practices it adopts, and these are always an enactment of intention. Frontiers, for example, are always purposeful, and the purpose they serve is always unambiguous, simple and apparently emerges in such a neat way that it could only be preconceived. Even when conceived as a source of threat, frontiers are calculated means of the containment of both populations and possible enemies: "Modern states used mutually agreed borders to gain controls over their peoples, and across the frontier were other states with which one might well be at war in the future. Imperial frontiers were designed to keep barbarian tribes at bay" (Hirst, 2005, p. 77). With such a conception of unmediated yet impersonal collective intention, how could any society be viewed as other than a military society?

Even when it acknowledges the violent or anti-democratic tendencies of such a view of society, this kind of Clausewitzian account always ends in resignation to the current status of international relations. In Hirst's account of contemporary world governance, states endure as both the most important international actors and sources of legitimacy (pp. 42–3). His intention here, as elsewhere, is to deflate what he sees as extravagant accounts of globalisation, which view the state as losing its initiative as the driver of international events.

This issue is outside of the purview of the present study. What is of interest is the persistent rhetoric of how it could really be no other way. This is not to say that there are not distinct advantages to the role of states, nor that they may play a significant role in democracy, nor even to say that Hirst is wrong. My point is simply that a view of the world in which social groups are identified purely as the subjects of strategic action will inevitably see the current state of world affairs as simply the result of what strategic rivalry has brought, and thus as inevitable and unquestionable, however this conclusion may be rationalised. Strategy is itself always seen as pragmatic and its results must be all that was practicable. What else could possibly have happened? Because he conceived of the collective social actor more in terms of a tension that needed to be managed, Clausewitz himself had a more complex view of what the results of violence might be. This sense of the volatility of the social group at war has not always descended to those who cite him.

Global war

As we have seen, with our account of those recent thinkers who apply a kind of Clausewitzian argument, the most common contemporary understanding of the relationship between war and civil society is to see the difference between the two disappearing. Zygmunt Bauman provides another account of the loss of difference between war and civil society in his discussion of the relationship between war and globalisation. This account pre-dates The War on Terror, and is an attempt to define the future of the nation state, which Bauman sees as no longer capable of fulfilling the security role assigned to it after 1648. The states that emerged from behind the vast security alliances of the Cold War were "in a state of advanced incapacitation" (Bauman, 2001, p. 12), unable to advance their own agendas for security, economic sustainability and cultural self-sufficiency. They were no longer states as this term had been understood since the Treaty of Westphalia. Global, particularly economic, forces override national boundaries without there being adequate global institutions capable of monitoring or checking their operation (p. 14).

In this environment, two types of wars have emerged, what Bauman calls "globalising wars," and "globalisation-induced wars." The former target nuisance states who do not respect the consensus that facilitates the progressive liberalisation of the global economy (p. 16). Unlike earlier wars, the aim here is to police unruly or obstructionist states, not to conquer territory. Holding territory is expensive and entangles the military in complex social and cultural situations that it cannot control or often even understand. Bauman writes, "The intention behind the decision to go to war is to throw the heretofore closed territory wide open to the global circulation of capital, money and commodities" (p. 16). Bauman's argument here is Clausewitzian, and he has evoked Clausewitz pretty automatically in the abstract of his essay.

Globalisation-induced wars, on the other hand, are not instrumental, but symptomatic. What they reveal, more than anything else, is the generalised anxiety caused by the loss of social and cultural anchoring all societies and subjectivities experience under globalisation:

> Unanchored trust desperately seeking shelter is a source of permanent anxiety. It prompts rising demands for certainty, security and safety. With the prospects of certainty and security dim and (in the context of global figuration devoid of a legible institutional frame for political intervention) and hopelessly beyond the grasp of individual or collective action, the pressures generated by ambient anxiety condense into the demand for more safety.
>
> (Bauman, 2001, p. 20)

These demands are felt at the level of the household and neighbourhood, where there is massive investment in locks and alarms, and demands for more and more policing. It is even felt at the level of the individual body where we administer on ourselves regimens of exercise and diet that to Bauman evince an intense anxiety about control and infiltration. To Bauman, there is only one short step from this anxiety about the insinuation of menace into the putative interior of our lives to a dream of social simplification: a dream that security can only be found in like adhering to like: "running to safety is guided by the dream of simplification. The reduction of variety looks like the best way to facilitate control" (Bauman, 2001, p. 21). Hence, the wars of ethnic solidarity in the Balkans in the 1990s, the wars that, of course, loomed over Bauman at the time he was writing this essay.

Several questions can be raised about this account. First, it is implied that something has been lost in the process of globalisation which did provide some sense of security. It seems that this was the accountability of institutions charged with defending the free expression of the citizenry and the integrity of the state. The idea that such institutions operated or that civilian populations were satisfied with them seems chimerical at best. Similarly, cultural anchoring is only ever known when it is lost. In the face of massive change, it is argued that our disorientation is the result of our having lost, what, in fact, we might never have thought of ourselves as having in the first place. The model of collective subjectivity here is a classically modern one in which we do not know the hidden truth of who we are till we feel the pressure of its loss or dysfunction.

This non-self-awareness is made most manifest by the claim that what happens in immediate situations is not the result of immediate causes but of global events. People engaged in ethnic disputes are enacting global political forces of which they are totally ignorant. There is a curious ethnic bias here. Global wars, as fought by global powers, are instrumental. The people who perpetrate them have agency and subjectivity. Globalisation is a strategy they are implementing for reasons they understand and advantages they can measure. Globalisation-induced wars, on the other hand, are symptomatic. Globalisation is merely a context the people who perpetrate these wars are ignorant of. If they understood it, they would not act as they do. They would seek ways of addressing the massive structure itself. Instead, they childishly chose to slaughter each other like ignorant armies clashing by night.

This leads to the final point: the links between the kinds of ethnic wars Bauman describes and globalisation do not seem necessary at all. As we know, the world has moved on to whole other genres of warfare that now require a more nuanced account and whose relationship with globalisation is not at all simple. What must have seemed the logical unfolding of an inevitable process now seems not so straightforward. The attempt to see Western body-shape anxiety and multi-ethnic wars as analogous to one another seems to enforce the view that to Bauman, there was a single global tendency, felt in the gyms of Brooklyn and the killing-fields of Bosnia in fairly similar ways. Post-September 11, 2001, it is harder to sustain the argument that globalisation is such a monolithic phenomenon. Yet Bauman insists on this point, arguing that indeed, despite their differences, wars of globalisation and globalisation-induced wars are really part of the one development part of "an intimate collaboration and mutual reinforcement" (Bauman, 2001, p. 25) of one another.

Bauman's argument is part of the common impulse to see war and civil society as becoming increasingly indistinct from one another. The unfolding of the global economy brings wars with it, as either an instrument of its development or a necessary by-product of the ferment it causes. If your ethos is one of social criticism, it is highly seductive to see these two as becoming one: we have seen this temptation played out in a variety of forms. Of course, it could never be possible that war and civil society have no relationship with one another. Yet, accounts that insist that this relationship simply involves the disappearance of the difference between them seem unable to convincingly explain or describe how their possible co-ordination is accompanied by an inevitable and under-estimated disjunction between them.

Jean Baudrillard develops an argument that also draws on Clausewitz, and attempts, like Bauman, to link war with the anxiety and solipsism seen to characterise contemporary Western social life. It also tries to develop a logic of opposition, here between the putatively more authentic wars of the past and the mediated wars of the present. His most important contribution, however, is to place war in the context of global media culture. Yet, again, as we will see, what is revealed is a warfare riven by its own challenge to itself. The obligatory reference to Clausewitz in Baudrillard's controversial *The Gulf War Did Not Take Place* (1991) is laden with irony. The Gulf War is a non-war, and "non-war is the absence of politics pursued by other means" (Baudrillard, 1995, p. 83). Hirst does not have a lot of time for Baudrillard's argument, like a lot of other people. It seems manifestly absurd, even childish and obnoxious, to describe as a non-war or non-event a war in which thousands of people died in a battle pursued by high-tech weapons for the control of territory as a means of gaining strategic advantage and dictating terms to your enemy. Many of these criticisms caricature Baudrillard's argument, failing to acknowledge his acknowledgement of the war's intensity and murderousness (Baudrillard, 1995, pp. 49–50). Nevertheless, the account of the war he gives is high-handed, written as if the war is merely an event in the media schedule of a sophisticated Western media audience, and is to be judged primarily on those terms. The dislocation of communities, the destruction of families, the truncation of individual lives in this as in any war were real by any definition of the term, and the reflexive nod to the suffering of the other in the context of an essay that speaks ironically about war does not do much to dispel the impression that this book is as much a product of Western narcissism and selfishness as the century of bungled and duplicitous imperial and post-imperial policy that lead to the war itself.

Notwithstanding this, the book makes some real contributions to a discussion of contemporary war. In fact, its key arguments spring less from an analysis of the media representation of war than from a discussion of how it revealed the present state of warfare. "War is no longer what it used to be," Baudrillard writes (1995, p. 85). It is war itself that is at stake here (p. 32). As in Virilio, there is a certain weird nostalgism in Baudrillard's account. Wars used to be real and were determined by strategic and material imperatives, Baudrillard implies. Now, war seems unreal. What is happening off-stage—in the media editing suites and the political control-rooms—no longer merely reflects or guides what is happening on the battle-field. The material war is merely a theatre in which pre-programmed strategies are played out. The war is a ritual game, therefore, used to make a point. It is not an honest contest of arms. What happens is not being determined on the battle-field, but is being organised as a spectacle that will reinforce certain truisms about the New World Order, announced to be the consequence of the end of the Cold War. In his discussion of the War on Terror, in *The Spirit of Terrorism*, Baudrillard puts this point even more emphatically when he argues that "real" war has become a mere adjunct of the media event. He writes,

> the real is superadded to the image like a bonus of terror, like an additional frisson: not only is it terrifying, but, what is more, it is real. Rather than the violence of the real being there first, and the frisson of the image being added to it, the image is there first, and the frisson of the real is added.
>
> (Baudrillard, 2002, p. 29)

The logic of deterrence that had defined the Cold War has become generalised. In a culture of decaffeinated coffee, safe sex and alcohol-free drinking, this new style of war reflects the creeping abstraction and virtualisation of all things:

> It is neither the strong form nor the degree zero of war, but the weak or phthisical degree, the asymptotic form which allows a brush with war but no encounter, the transparent degree which allows war to be seen from the depths of the darkroom...we have fallen into

soft war...as though the irruption or the event of war had become obscene and insupportable, no longer sustainable, like every real event moreover. Everything therefore is transposed into the virtual, and we are confronted with a virtual apocalypse.

(Baudrillard, 2002, pp. 26–7)

The war then is really being fought in a domain of abstract possibility, rather than on the field of physical competition. This virtualisation of war is part of the general virtualisation of all things in post-modern society, in which the hyper-real logic of representation becomes the primary site of human interaction. In the end, war becomes a pre-programmed run-through of completely predictable gestures. It becomes a non-war whose abstraction coincides with material violence (Baudrillard, 2002, pp. 49–50), but a war whose centre of gravity and meaning is off the battlefield nonetheless. What we witness then is not a pragmatic pursuit of strategic ends through physical means, but a kind of "technological mannerism" (p. 34), an "abstract operation," not measured against the capacity of an enemy, but against its own logic (p. 45), a "programmed unfolding" (p. 57), an "unreal made-to-order victory" (p. 73). The war "no longer proceeds from a political will to dominate or from a vital impulsion or an antagonistic violence, but from the will to impose a general consensus by deterrence" (p. 83). This derealisation was already at work in all Western democracies, and reflects a vanilla conception of warfare, indeed of power, as something clean and virtuous (p. 56): no ragtag, messy, unpredictable violence here in which ascendancy is to be allowed to the stronger in a contest. Victory must be pre-programmed as the inevitable triumph of a dispassionate power, whose truth and virtue must be acknowledged and accepted.

The implication here is that war was once an unadorned and brave meeting of strengths, whose symbolic dimensions were merely superadded to it, and that the situation has now been reversed. As we have seen throughout this study, however, war is distinguished from mere violence, even collective purposeful violence, by its grounding in varied but specific logics of social meaning. Its function has always been to enact certain understandings of the nature of the society it purports to defend. Leaving aside the obvious point that any contest of arms, no matter how unduplicitous and honest it may be, remains the most vicious way of organising human relations, it seems naïve to assume that war was ever less than heavily symbolic or ritual.

Nevertheless, what Baudrillard's account offers is an updated, post-modern version of what we have been investigating all along. He may be naïve to write of it as if it is something new, and imply that once upon a time these things were sorted out fairly by real men. In fact, the achievement of his argument should be that war has never been a mere contest of arms, and that it finds its meaning in and through the structures of the society it activates and by the way in which it is represented. In the Gulf War and the War on Terror, we see this complex in its contemporary form, in which it is globalism itself, the hegemonic system of world economic, cultural and political organisation, which generates war within itself. To Baudrillard, the War on Terror is "the only really global [war], since what is at stake is globalisation itself" (Baudrillard, 2002, p. 11). He continues,

> With each succeeding war, we have moved further towards a single world order. Today that order, which has virtually reached its culmination, finds itself grappling with the antagonistic forces scattered throughout the very heartlands of the global, in all the current convulsions. A fractal war of all cells, all singularities, revolting in the form of antibodies...It is what haunts every world order, all hegemonic domination—if Islam dominated the world, terrorism would rise against Islam, *for it is the world, the globe itself, which resists globalisation.*
>
> (Baudrillard, 2002, p. 12)

Like Žižek, whom we will study below, Baudrillard sees the US attempt to counter terrorism by invasions of Afghanistan and Iraq as attempts to revive conventional warfare and its fantasies. The system of global order necessarily generates attacks on itself as a consequence of its homogenisation of the world. It then mounts a war in the attempt to reinstitute the fantasy of the neat, symmetrical opposition of two rival parties. The aim of the war is to "save war" itself, but more importantly the moral symbolics of war, to quickly conceal the true global situation behind the routine mythologies of war. But war "merely offers a rehash of the past, with the same deluge of military forces, bogus information, senseless bombardment, emotive and deceitful language, technological deployment and brainwashing" (Baudrillard, 2002, p. 42). War, far from restoring the real from behind, before or beyond the artificiality and virtuality of post-modernism, is an attempt to restore the illusions of Western dominance, morality and initiative. The progressive West labours again to save the benighted world. Yet, the counter-force the West imagines is not coming from the darkened, primitive regions which need to be saved from themselves, and drawn into the light, if only they would give up on their traditions and realise the benefits of globalisation. The counter-movement is the West's globalisation: "The West, in the position of God (divine omnipotence and absolute moral legitimacy) has become suicidal, and declared war on itself" (Baudrillard, 2002, p. 7). Here, war is its own counter-movement. Like Virilio, Baudrillard imagines contemporary war in terms of an opposition. For Virilio, it had been between the immediacy of war and the extended time of political decision-making. For Baudrillard, it is the difference between authentic and mediated conflict. This is, of course, a naïve even imaginary opposition. Yet, what is important is that the argument actually leads somewhere else; towards an image of contemporary war as its own undoing. Again, beneath the logic of opposition is a conception of war as something much more complex and entangled.

The platitude that, in the contemporary world, the difference between war and its other, usually understood as rational and democratic civil society, is disappearing usually relies, as we have seen, on an un-interrogated adoption of the Clausewitzian view, understood in a way very foreign to Clausewitz himself: as social critique. Hardt and Negri's *Multitude* provides another example of this argument, which it too connects with globalisation. For Hardt and Negri, the globalised world has produced the inter-locking co-ordination of a neo-liberal hegemony in which state power, corporations and NGO's form a single regime, subject to a consistent unidirectional and resolutely unjust policy. This undeclared Empire is distinguished from traditional conceptions of empire by its abstraction. It is not a localised power traceable to a cosmopolitan centre, but instead a "network power," operating in informal and invisible multiple connections as much as through explicit institutions of power. This imperial power is matched by the thorough and ubiquitous administration of individual bodies and lives, long identified by Foucault and Agamben as biopower. War extends the oversight of empire across the globe; while biopower intensifies it within what we conventionally understood as societies. Under Empire, war has become "a general phenomenon, global and interminable" (Hardt and Negri, 2004, p. 3). Today's wars are not wars as we conventionally understand them. If the world is now increasingly a single imperial system, then the wars that are taking place across the world should no longer be considered in terms of the organised conflicts between states that have defined war in the post-Westphalian world. Current wars are better understood as global civil wars, rifts within a single political entity, not struggles between different entities (p. 3).

The use of these wars in the organisation of Empire has eroded the difference between war and peace till the two are indistinguishable. The loss of distinction between the inside and the outside of society erodes the distinction between warfare and policing (p. 21). As has been widely commented upon, and as we have noted ourselves, techniques of warfare and policing converge: police forces have para-military units, such as SWAT teams, whose equipment, organisation, uniforms and ways of operating mimic the military. Similarly, social policies are described and imagined as wars. Citing and adapting Clausewitz, Hardt and Negri write that under this regime, where empire extends its power by warfare and administers its societies in a para-military way, then war "is becoming the primary organising principle of society" (Hardt and Negri, 2004, p. 12). The distinction between friendship and enmity becomes untenable, as alliances and pseudo-alliances form in the name of weak coalitions like the one formed to invade Iraq in 2003 (p. 15), and the distinction between fighting and peacekeeping also becomes confused, since the same soldiers perform both roles, sometimes apparently at the same time (p. 52). The goal of this loss of difference between war and peace is the total subordination of society to the organisation of war:

> The domestic face of just-war doctrines and the war against terrorism is a regime aimed at near complete social control, which some authors describe as a passage from a welfare state to a warfare state and others characterise as a so-called zero-tolerance society. This is a society whose diminishing civil liberties and increasing rates of incarceration are in certain respects a manifestation of a constant social war.
> (Hardt and Negri, 2004, p. 17)

The bulk of *Multitude* is given over to a discussion of how this regime can be resisted. There is difference within Empire, a resistance to its logic of homogenisation. This is the loose but rich potential of the multiple and plural multitude of the world's populations, on whom the hierarchies of Empire are being imposed. No longer to be conceived of as the masses, or the proletariat, and no longer to be seen as a unified political body, multitude joins vastly different segments of the human population into networks comparable and rival to Empire's own network power. The multitude is already engaged in a wide range of forms of dissent and resistance:

> Throughout modernity, and still today, resistance movements have had to confront war and the violence it imposes, sometimes with and sometimes without violent means. Perhaps we should say rather that the

great wars of liberation are (or should be) oriented ultimately towards a "war against war," that is, an active effort to destroy the regime of violence that perpetuates our state of war and supports the systems of inequality and oppression. This is a condition necessary for realising the democracy of the multitude.

(Hardt and Negri, 2004, p. 67)

There is an internal difference possible within the regime of total social war and that difference is activated by the democratic politics of the multitude. It is this politics that offers us the opportunity of defeating war. Yet, this difference is imagined as itself a kind of warfare. The opposition to war is war.

The challenge for these post-Clausewitzian accounts that argue for a collapse of difference between war and peace is to translate the anger and anguish of rhetorical accusation into a meaningful model of society. Social administration may ape warfare, yet within societies, the difference between even this warfare and something else in social relations—peace, love, trust, relationship—remains alive. Accounts of the loss of difference between war and peace must take account of this difference, if they are to be useful in elucidating exactly how warfare operates in relation to its other. Hardt and Negri offer such a difference in the figure of the multitude but in the concept of the "war against war," they take it back again. We need to resist war, because war is a form of total social control, and a servant and facilitator of inequality, injustice and atrocity. Yet the action of the multitude is to be represented itself as warfare! In this account, salvation from war is war.

It is not necessarily that what is different to war is simply to be preserved and enlarged in order to resist war. We cannot get that far yet. Yet that difference does at least need to be understood, if we are to get anywhere in understanding what war really is. Our problem is not that there is a loss of difference between war and peace, but that the difference itself—in the form of wars fought for peace, or on behalf of human rights—serves war. In this way, Hardt and Negri's account is part of the problem not part of the solution.

Recovering difference

It is not simply wrong to argue that the difference between war and its other is disappearing. There is plenty of evidence for the overlap between the practices of war and the practices of peace in the contemporary world. Yet, this view is not complete or complex enough to provide a truly telling insight into the problem of war, especially in its current form. I want now to turn to a series of thinkers who, while acknowledging the inter-penetration of war and its other in the contemporary world, have also provided a more nuanced account of how that complex is experienced or what it might mean.

Although he includes the War on Terror in his discussion, to Achille Mbembe, it is the colonial war that is the archetype of the state of war in the contemporary. In Mbembe, the distinction between war and peace, as well as between state and non-state combatants, has broken down, leaving the identity of war itself in crisis. This is the flipside of the crisis of the thinking of the social we derived at the end of our discussion of Derrida. The increasing difficulty of defining a clear distinction between war and its other produces a crisis in the definition of war as much as of the social.

Mbembe's aim is to reveal a style of sovereignty whose function is not the achievement of political autonomy, but "the generalised instrumentalisation of human existence and the material destruction of human bodies and populations" (Mbembe, 2003, p. 14). He thus goes beyond accounts of sovereignty as the state of exception, arguing that this is a mere preliminary to the exercise of a "right to kill" (p. 16). Sovereignty then creates "*death-worlds*, new and unique forms of social existence in which vast populations are subjected to conditions of life conferring on them the status of living dead" (p. 40). Mbembe argues that one of the central critiques of modernity has focussed on the "complete conflation of war and politics" (p. 18), identified with Nazism. The historical origins of the logic the Nazis put into practice, however, is to be found in colonialism. The colonial—and later apartheid systems— gave rise to a "unique terror formation" displaying a "concatenation of biopower, the state of exception and the state of siege" (p. 22). Mbembe goes on: "the colony represents the site where sovereignty consists fundamentally in the exercise of a power outside the law...and where 'peace' is more likely to take on the face of a 'war without end'" (p. 23). In this context, "the distinction between war and peace does not avail" (p.25). Colonial war does not simply aim at the pacification of the colony. War – whether enacted through explicit armed conflict or through the uninterrupted terrorisation of the local population, or through processes of administration that divide communities, uproot crops and orchards, hold populations in indefinite bureaucratic paralysis (at permit offices and check-points), disable economic relationships or explicitly arrest, detain and kill arbitrarily – becomes colonial normality. "The fiction of a distinction between 'the ends of war' and 'the means of war' collapses" (p. 25).

Mbembe evokes Deleuze and Guattari's trope of the "war-machine" to describe the related death-world where warfare has become dissociated from the state. He uses Africa as an example:

> Here, the political economy of statehood dramatically changed over the last quarter of the twentieth century. Many African states can no longer claim a monopoly on violence and on the means of coercion within their territory. Nor can they claim a monopoly on territorial boundaries. Coercion itself has become a market commodity. Military manpower is bought and sold on a market in which the identity of suppliers and purchasers means almost nothing. Urban militias, private armies, armies of regional lords, private security firms, and state armies all claim the right to exercise violence or to kill. Neighbouring states or rebel movements lease armies to poor states. Nonstate deployers of violence supply two critical coercive resources: labour and minerals. Increasingly, the vast majority of armies are composed of citizen soldiers: child soldiers, mercenaries and privateers.
> (Mbembe, 2003, p. 32)

We have witnessed how such arrangements, entangled with struggles over resources destined for western markets, from diamonds to the opium poppy, quickly establish themselves in regions where the state has been destabilised and becomes only a bit-player, like Afghanistan and Iraq. It would be naïve to see such a model becoming generalised directly, but given that the consequences of climate change remain unpredictable, and the tenor of Mbembe's argument is that what happens in the post-colonial world might be repeated in the supposedly developed world (colony prefigures camp), it would be foolish therefore to dismiss these developments as of only local interest.

Herfried Münkler picks up this very point in an account of *The New Wars*. Citing Trutz von Throta, Münkler speculates about whether the present state of war in Africa might say more about the future of the developed world than its past (Münkler, 2005, p. 34). The analogy between an autonomous, self-motivating and more or less continuous war that simply feeds off itself and the War on Terror—let alone the wars declared in western societies on drugs, crime, poverty and so on—is hard to resist. How does Münkler characterise these wars? They are first and foremost wars without noticeable beginning and achievable end. "They begin *somehow or other*, and end *somewhere or other*. Scarcely any of the parties can say clearly which purposes and aims are being pursued by means of the war" (p. 33). Many of the processes of the legitimate daylight global economy and culture feed this propensity to war. The new wars are fed by their "insertion into the process of economic globalisation or shadow globalisation, and the development of new constellations of interests geared not to the ending of war but to its theoretically endless continuation" (pp. 32–3). The distinction between combatants and non-combatants breaks down (p. 15), exposing women in particular to a sexual violence now used unambiguously as a weapon of terror and ethnic domination. Indeed, Münkler draws attention to "the extensive sexualisation of violence that is observable in nearly all the new wars" (p. 86). Strategic goals fade in the face of an "economy…of violence…one big torture machine whose purpose is to produce pain and suffering but not to enforce a political will" (p. 86).

This development in which war has become a self-generating activity is perhaps the most explicit repudiation we have met of Clausewitz's instrumentalist account of warfare. Again, Münkler reads it as symptomatic of a structural crisis in contemporary sociality. The supposed modern rules of warfare, established at the end of the Thirty Years' War, in which states co-existed inside agreed boundaries and exercised a monopoly on violence within their own territory, are really what is at stake in the new wars. A generalised and irregular warfare, which preceded the formation of the state, now returns at the other end of the period of rational warfare, where the state is starting to break down:

> [T]here is also the question of whether [the new wars] can in a sense be described as a return to a stage prior to Europe's early modern statization of war; a look at that earlier period is a suitable way of bringing out similarities with the conditions in which the state is *no longer* what it was then *not yet*: the monopolist of war.
> (Münkler, 2005, p. 2)

This spread of war sweeps up even the organisations whose aim is to bring peace, such as international aid agencies, which get caught up in the economy of war by making resources available that can swiftly end up on the black market: "what was supposed to relieve hunger and poverty becomes a resource of war" (p. 18). Yet, this model of a continuous war "with neither an identifiable beginning or a clearly defined end" (p. 15) also describes wars in which states are now engaged. The war in Iraq and the War on Terror, as well as the generalised use of warfare as the language of social policy, see the limits of the instrumentalist account of war. Torture, extraordinary rendition, imprecise bombing, rape, as well as the intensification of police action, legislation to restrict press freedom and civil and human rights more generally, all see the state spreading terror, executing arbitrary power, cultivating heightened social division and insinuating suspicion into social relations. It is, of course, arguable that this has always been a resource to which the state has easily and readily turned, and Derrida, for example, has argued that all states are by definition "rogue states" (Derrida, 2005). However, what we see now is not the use of these techniques in pursuit of specific social goals (economic, geopolitical or racial domination, for example), but as a substitute for sociality in general, in a social, even global, war without term. Terror becomes not a tool, but a form of continuous tension, from which some may profit, while others remain cowed. As Mbembe's description of the Israeli occupation of Palestine outlines, this kind of war soon becomes normalised, a state of constant intimidation and emergency. The wars on drugs and crime that have dominated social policy in certain western countries achieve nothing more than this state of permanent unsettling of the social order.

Here, we see the historical realisation of a non-Clausewitzian version of war. The generalisation of war as a type of peace with peace's aims shows that the deconstruction of the war/peace and friend/enemy dichotomies we have outlined in Derrida is not simply a piece of abstruse theorising. The historical situation in which we live is not one where war and its other are clear alternatives. Given we are in a perpetual state of low-level conflict in which acts of war and the rhetoric of the social combine with one another in complex ways, it is chimerical to even believe that the tangle can be rationalised into discrete alternatives wherein we can actually withdraw our troops, pressure our governments, discipline our corporations and pacify our popular culture in order to construct an enduring peace. As we have seen, this tangle persists in our understandings of what society is, even when they attempt to simplify it. Mbembe and Münkler show that this situation is not merely theoretical.

It is thus too simple to see this complex state of affairs as simply the implementation of policy, as the widespread reference to Clausewitz would imply, nor as merely the erasure of difference between war and its other. The generalisation of war as Mbembe and Münkler describe it reveals a world in which the intensification of war in one place—one part of the world or fraction of society—has as its aim the consolidation of peace in another. Violence in the occupied zone or the failed state coincides with the uninhibited extension of luxury and security elsewhere. The sacralisation of the victims of the September 11 attacks, when viewed in a global context, is evidence of a society unable to believe that the violence it was accustomed to witness, even enact, elsewhere could be visited on its very heartland. The sense of outrage, even injustice, this provoked is illustrative of a global situation where violence is normalised but not evenly spread. The spreading administration of violence in one place is the securing of peace elsewhere, and it is this very contradiction that allows the violence to be rationalised. This then confirms the deconstructive account in which war and peace only attain their co-ordination because of the irreducible disjunction between them.

Alain Badiou takes up this point in an account of how war's aim is to deploy a violence that guarantees luxury elsewhere. His account is less to do with the social administration that is co-ordinated with war, than with the reconfiguration of the experience of time under US global hegemony. Badiou argues that "war has been what historically attests to the present" (Badiou, 2006, p. 36). He gives three reasons for this. First, in the West, both modern and post-modern understandings of historical time have consistently used the Second World War as their reference point: events are described as "pre-war" and "post-war", as if only war itself is present to itself, the thing that all other events either anticipate or follow. Secondly, war is seen as playing a decisive and deterministic role in the constitution of the nature of the present, and thirdly, by constructing a moment outside of normal peaceful human interaction, war contrives a "fraternal...community outside the normal rules" (pp. 36–7).

The wars taking place now, on the other hand, do not interrupt the normal sequence of world events. Instead, they insist on the great continuity of Western power and self-satisfaction. Badiou writes,

> The aim of these wars is to protect, to endure, and for this reason to destroy anything that is not homogeneous with this duration, and this protection—protection of "Western" comfort, of measured enjoyment. They are wars that are totally sterile with respect to the order of time.
>
> (Badiou, 2006, p. 37)

Here, we have an argument reminiscent of Martin Shaw's point in *The New Western Way of War*, that in the contemporary situation, Western societies will not tolerate a war that in any way destabilises or complicates normal (especially economic) life. Badiou connects this refusal of the interruption of Western luxury with the American belief in the limitlessness of its entitlement and power. "[T]he metaphysics of

American power is a metaphysics of the unlimited," he writes, "for the USA, there are no limits" (Badiou, 2006, p. 45). The US force must be seen as irresistible.

War thus enters into a dehistoricised space, becoming atemporal and reflexive, automatic, a mere indication of a global system invulnerable to dispute. In this way, it is not connected to any of the dialectics that may have located it in specific historical situations, and in which it may have contributed, albeit negatively, to progress. The key instance here is the war/revolution dialectic:

> [F]rom 1917 to 1976 (Mao's death), war and revolution constituted the transcendental regime of the present. Of this present, which bound together the localised force of war and the remote becoming of emancipation, nothing remains that might be activated at the moment...We are now in a limbo world, suspended between an old, inactive dialectical figure (war and/or revolution), and a false commercial and military present that seeks to protect its future by dispensing with the present, and by erasing everything of the past, that was, in the past, in the present.
>
> (Badiou, 2006, p. 38)

War is thus an administration of power, rather than a fatal hiatus between normal constituted socially stable epochs. A symptom of this is the fact that wars are no longer declared. The declaration of war attested to the specificity and accidental quality of war as an event. War is now a general state, not a specific episode. It is this that makes war and peace "indistinguishable" (p. 40).

Badiou also provides an account of the relationship between the combatants in the War on Terror that shows a deep continuity, even within opposition. He describes the relationship between the United States and Al-Qaida as one of "the disjunctive synthesis of two nihilisms" (p. 31). This relationship is a synthesis because "the principal actors are of the same kind," both belonging to a world of wealth and power, and of "the arrogance of self-certitude based on the void" (p. 31). It is disjunctive because these two antagonists seek each other through crime. This notion does not only restore the idea of difference to warfare, something glibly wished away in endlessly vituperative contemporary accounts of war and peace, it also provides a model of how war should be seen as a deep collaboration in which two partners build a single structure while trying to annihilate one another. Enemies are at work on the same project, even if its aim is mutual destruction. In this sense, the logic of war as a self-contained thing comes into question, especially if this thing is seen as a binary opposition between two mutually exclusive parties. Badiou reminds us that fighting itself is the simultaneous deployment of contradiction and collaboration.

The Clausewitzian accounts in which the difference between war and its others is seen to be disappearing are not then the only accounts of warfare in and after the era of the global. Slavoj Žižek, writing in the psychoanalytic tradition, presents an account of war post-September 11 attacks, that responds to some of the questions raised in Derrida's deconstruction of war. It is by way of this account that we will start to progress towards a conclusion.

Since the Gulf War of 1991, many like Baudrillard have argued that war has become virtual, indistinguishable from a computer game, robbed of its physical intensity, and the immediacy of the clash of hot bodies and hard metal and thus apparently disconnected from the horror of its consequences. The result of this is seen to be the increasing abstraction of its moral meaning: from bloody carnage to digital pulses that simply fade when neutralised, war has lost its material weight and thus its players' connection with its brutality. Concealed by euphemisms like collateral damage, rendered in the Revolution in Military Affairs (RMA), indistinguishable from other corporate technical projects, warfare through the 1990s was seen as increasingly physically and morally weightless. By showing how a high-tech army can get bogged down in an irregular insurgency, the second Gulf War has done much to show how chimerical the RMA actually was. Improvised weapons and putatively sectarian militias seem to have restored us to the material war we think more moral: where bodies are dragged through the streets and the failure of First World soldiers to secure any military or political progress ends in them taking recourse to rape and atrocity in a vicious attempt to restore their imagined right to dominance.

Yet the theme of "reality" needs a more detailed problematisation if we are to understand whether it is a useful term in evaluating war. It is not enough to argue that a technical reliance on representation as a means of gaining control of the battle-scene automatically relegates war to the fantastic. If this were the case, then military planning and education, from the strategic map to the general staff, would be seen to belong to the unreal. The relationship between "fantasy" and "reality" in the context of war needs more consideration. In his discussion of the terrorist attacks of September 11, 2001, *Welcome to the Desert of the Real,* Slavoj Žižek draws on Lacanian theory in order to provide such an account.

According to Žižek, the first moralistic responses to the terrorist attacks proposed that they represented the burst of historical reality into the self-indulgent fantasy world of post-modern luxury in which the West, and especially the United States, were seen to be wallowing. Yet to Žižek, what was apparent was not the intrusion of the real into the collective fantasy, but the opposite: the attacks were a repetition of what was so familiar from fantasy: "It is not that reality entered our image: the image entered and shattered our reality (i.e. the symbolic coordinates which determine what we experience as reality)" (Žižek, 2002, p. 16). Westerners are accustomed to seeing atrocity and violence as something that happens elsewhere, and that appears only in their media. Violence belongs to the domain of the image, not the harsh brutality of what we normally consider reality. Reality, in the ordinary sense, is merely a consensus built from consistently validated symbolic co-ordinates that we agree to take as impersonally verified. As long as it remains undisturbed this consistency in the symbolic order suffices for us as if it were unmediated, literal fact. Yet, according to Lacan, behind or beyond this consensual reality lies a domain of more pressing and profound intensity, the Real. "In our daily existence, we are immersed in 'reality'... and this immersion is disturbed by symptoms which bear witness to the fact that another, repressed level of our psyche resists this immersion" (Žižek, 2002, p. 17). The Real has been connected with the irrepressibility of the unconscious or the irreducibility of the bodily. In Žižek's account, the Real emerges not primarily by way of this physicality, but through fantasy itself. The Real so contests our normal sense of what is real that we can only deal with it by packaging it in fantasy:

> *precisely because it is real, that is, on account of its traumatic/excessive character, we are unable to integrate it into (what we experience as) reality, and are therefore compelled to experience it as a nightmare apparition.* This is what the compelling image of the collapse of the WTC was: an image, a semblance, an "effect," which, at the same time, delivered "the thing itself."
>
> (Žižek, 2002, p. 17)

The material violence on which the world order of Western ascendancy depends is a Real so horrible it can only be engaged with by way of the structure of fantasy. The reference point for Žižek here is the Hollywood blockbusters (p. 16) in which skyscrapers implode and freeways become sites of carnage, confusion and blockage, flirtations with the abject violence that commodified fantasy keeps only a flicker of light away.

The fantasy reveals the Real to us by structuring our repressed psychic investments. It is the emergence of the Real that the images of the collapsing towers provided.

The Real, however, is not a place where our truth offers us deliverance and comfort. The Real remains a site of horror. This is why we can only engage with it by way of fantasy. It cannot be met directly in an unmediated fashion. Our experience of this truth is vertiginous, and we seek to escape it as quickly as possible. We want our consensual reality to return so that we can be protected from the Real. This is what we seek in counter-attack, why September 11 led to a "war on terror." The function of this strategy is symbolic. Its aim is not necessarily to achieve knowable material goals or if it is these are accompanied by a larger goal: to restore the co-ordinates of that symbolic consensus we know as our reality and that the Real has shattered.

The Real then shatters our consensual reality, and our first reaction is to rush to restore that reality by reanimating one of our collective illusions: the efficacy of maximum force, for example, or the belief that the most liberal economy naturally entails a liberal justice that can and should be imposed on a society from the outside. Interestingly, however, Žižek does not romanticise the political potential of the Real. He does not simply see the Real as performing some subversive function. How could there be a positive politics of the Real, when the Real's most important effects are made felt simply as interruptions? The political use of the Real is in the reaction to it, therefore, and it cannot be seen as able to be co-ordinated with any progressive programme, or really any progress at all. The function of the Real is to encourage and even justify the restoration of the illusory reality it has disturbed. He writes, "the Real Thing is a fantasmatic spectre whose presence guarantees the consistency of our symbolic edifice" (Žižek, 2002, p. 32). Conservative politics evokes the Real therefore as the thing that threatens the symbolic order, and against which we need protection. Such a logic could, of course, be used in a reading of Hobbes as psychological fantasy: sovereignty organises a political order whose function is to wall out an unknowable violence that was never literally experienced as such, but looms as the imaginary outside of our social systems, always threatening to disrupt and ruin them.

War in Žižek, then, has a complex function. More than a battleground on which armies struggle to assure the strategic and economic advantage of the societies they represent, it is the site of a struggle over *reality*. Intense violence disrupts consensual reality and discloses the Real; as a counter-attack, organised warfare aims to restore the consistency of the reality that has been disturbed and is necessary to protect us from the horror of the Real of the unthinkable, the physical and the unconscious. War then is both the outside of society threatening its consistency and restoring that consistency. In it, the coherence of the social is both threatened and protected. This is not to say simply that individual societies are attacked by the violence of their enemies and use violence to protect themselves. It is not an individual society that is threatened and defended by war, but sociality, the very nature of the social itself. The collective violence of war is thus both the most social and anti-social force. Perhaps here we find an answer to the question we asked at the end of our discussion of Derrida: Does the aporetic nature of war presented in the deconstruction of the friend/enemy binary require a rethinking of the nature of the social, in order for us to conceive of a sociality without war? In Žižek's account, it seems that the rethinking of sociality itself, the very debate deconstruction would encourage is itself to be identified with war. War is a rethinking of the limits of the social. The rethinking of the limits of the social exposes us to war.

An example of how this takes place emerges through Žižek's discussion of contemporary warfare in relation to Agamben's account of bare life. As is well known, Agamben sees political sovereignty as enacted in the reduction of certain people to the status of "bare life," a mere physical existence separate from civic identity and its associated rights and privileges. The concentration camp is the classical site of the operation of this sovereignty: the Jew, Romany, homosexual, dissident or disabled is reduced to a mere disposable object of social power to the point of killing. Žižek adapts this model to a reading of contemporary warfare. He writes,

> We no longer have wars in the old sense of a regulated conflict between sovereign states in which certain rules apply...What remains are two types of conflict: either struggles between groups of Homo sacer—"ethnic-religious conflicts" which violate the rules of universal human rights, do not count as wars proper, and call for "humanitarian pacifist" intervention by Western powers—or direct attacks on the USA or other representatives of the new global order, in which case, again, we do not have wars proper, merely "unlawful combatants" criminally resisting the forces of universal order.
> (Žižek, 2002, p. 93)

In the first of these cases, war takes place amongst groups already reduced to the status of bare life, having been excluded from global citizenship.

In the second, those who attack the West become bare life by being unrecognised as anything but a form of disposable deviance. The limit of the social is a resource of war and at war's disposal. War enacts what the social is to be by exclusion. To Žižek, this is indicative of the general state of post-politics in which we live, in which we "are all 'excluded' in the sense that our most elementary 'zero' position is that of an object of biopolitics, and that possible political and citizenship rights are given to us as a secondary gesture, in accordance with biopolitical strategic considerations" (Žižek, 2002, p. 95). We have seen throughout this study how war and the social are always defined in relation to one another: perhaps war is the thing that social order is constituted to withstand; perhaps war is continuous with the social; a third "economic" option saw war as both generated by and threatening the social at one and the same time. Following Derrida, we have seen the aporetic relationship between war and the social, where the two are simultaneously always in play in relation to one another. In Žižek, we see this as a politics: the social is not only enacted inevitably in war, but war is the continual rethinking of the limit of the social as the operation of power. Social identities—marginalised ethnic groups, political dissidents—emerge on the limits of the social as part of the operation of war, becoming objects of power. This is the inverse of the Hobbesian account in which rethinking the social inevitably exposes us to the risk of war. The history of thinking about war in relation to its other shows that war and the social are not thought of separately to one another.

The argument that there has been a collapse of difference between war and its other over-simplifies a more complex state of affairs. There is a rhetorical comfort in this kind of argument which presents itself as critique, and thus likes to refer to the Clausewitzian idea that war is actually the implementation of an intention: in this way, the generalisation of war can be represented as policy. Yet, it provides only half an insight, and allows the real problem to endure invisibly. The problem of war is peace, or more accurately, war's various others. Accounts like Mbembe's, Münkler's, Badiou's and Žižek's show that the generalisation of war is actually the consolidation of peace, even as fantasy, and thus not a collapse of difference, but its opposite, a radical and political differentiation in which war and its other are both intensified in relation to one another in the one act. It is thus this difference that is the problem.

Conclusion: War and Human Rights

The aim of this book has been to show that war is always defined in relation to something else, what we have called its other. This other may vary: it may be society, sovereign authority, politics, love, peace, friendship or something else. What is important about this relationship is not that it defines what war is opposite to and distinct from nor does it simply identify what the mechanism is that uses war as an instrument. It reveals the context within which war must emerge. This is not simply the historical or political context. Historical context is important, of course. Each thinker that we have studied can be said to be reacting to the specific war that defined or dominated their era: Hobbes, the religious and civil wars of the seventeenth century; Clausewitz, the wars of the revolutionary and Napoleonic era, in which the people became a major player for the first time; Freud, the First World War; Foucault, the war of the racial Holocaust; Virilio, the Cold War of Mutually Assured Destruction; Baudrillard, the First Gulf War; Žižek, the War on Terror and so on. Sometimes this address is direct and conscious; sometimes implicit and incidental. Their accounts, however, emerge in more than an historical context: they rely on a *conceptual* context as well, in which war is not just a literal material situation, but an abstraction or an idea. This is what makes war available as part of the unfolding of human meaning. In this way, war itself is not the problem. It is the way war is implicated in and required by other denominations of human meaning that condemns us to repeated bouts of official violence. War never emerges outside of a relationship to some conceptual other, and it is in the complexity of this relationship that our future fortunes of war will be determined.

As we have seen, this relationship can never be seen to stabilise simply around the idea that war and its other are opposites or merely continuous with one another. Even in the accounts of Hobbes and

Kant, for example, the idea that war and civil society are opposites proves to be a much more complex argument than it at first appears: in the Hobbesian version, we find that civil society may seem to supplant the natural state of war, but is in fact, the fulfilment of war's ostensible purposes. In Kant, peace emerges as a progression beyond war, but only by way of it. In both these arguments, the relationship between war and peace is not one of simple contrast, but of complex entanglement, in which peace never quite leaves war behind, indeed continues to depend on it. In our time, on the other hand, we see a kind of Clausewitzian consensus, in which war is seen as co-ordinated with both international diplomatic and domestic social policy, as a vast para-military police action in which unruly lapsed allies are disciplined or various kinds of social deviancy defined and excoriated. Theorists are quick to argue that what we see here is the increasing disappearance of any difference between war and its other. Yet, while this generalisation of war seems to be taking place, at no time has war been less publicly acceptable nor more automatically rejected—even indiscriminately and pre-emptively—by vast sections of the population. The generalised moral revulsion at war is not a real obstacle to war nor does it herald its demise. Indeed, while their constituents demonstrate against wars and ridicule them on blogs, politicians seem paralysed when it comes to contesting the determination of heads of government to resort to warfare. As Ryan C Hendrickson has argued in *The Clinton Wars: The Constitution, Congress and War Powers* (Hendrickson, 2002), the US Congress has been increasingly reluctant to resist the will of a president who has decided on military action, even when it has the constitutional power to do so. The general revulsion at war therefore is not necessarily incompatible with a generalisation of war in practice. Indeed, my aim has been to show the opposite: that the general deployment and the general rejection of war are part of a single complex. It is much too simple, however, to see this complex as part of a willing blindness on the part of the bulk of humanity, wherein moral comfort and self-regard would be assured by rejection of war even though affluent lifestyles may depend on war for their continued opportunity. It is too easy to see the war problem simply morally, that we play at rejecting wars from which we are actually happy to profit. Our rejection of war, like our purported commitment to democracy and human rights, is not merely hypocritical. It must be understood as part of a complex in which war and its other emerge together in a double relationship in which they both encourage and refuse one another: we reject war because it ruins social relations, shatters bodies and savages our human rights. Yet, we also look to war to preserve the social, protect threatened lives and enlarge rights. War kills and saves simultaneously. It destroys the things in the name of which it is implemented. To see a loss of difference between war and its other is to overlook the complex situations in which war emerges and which keep it alive despite our moral repugnance and endless official lamentations for those of us whom it has annihilated.

To say that war is double and that it is implicated conceptually in other values that we want to preserve is not to simply say that we should be resigned to war enduring. It is an attempt to provide a new and useful way by which war can be understood, and argues, as all analysis does, that material situations like war cannot be dealt with if they are not understood, and that new ways must continually be sought to rethink them. Theory is not an enduring ideal truth to be applied to practical situations, but the invention of new conceptual forms that may help us represent and explain hitherto obscure or enigmatic phenomena. Thinking of war in terms of the war/other complex means always seeing the emergence of war as the deployment of something else with it. The two must always appear in relationship with one another even if they are considered to be antagonistic or mutually destructive. So war and whatever its other might be in a particular context, facilitate the emergence of one another, even in their defiance of one another. It is this inseparability of war and its other that makes it possible to see war and its other as co-ordinated. What was Nazi war but a tribute, in its most organised and exultant murderousness, to life? What was Communist insurgency but the most regimented and anonymous embrace of the possibilities of freedom? And what are democracy's post-1989 wars but the most brutal and oppressive attempt to spread human rights?

These complex situations can and should not be disguised by an eternal but vacuous resort to morality. The logic that attributes the doubleness of war to hypocrisy is a singularly unenlightening example of the ascendancy of moral discourse in discussions of war. Of course, our attitude to war must be moral: we could not protect ourselves from the cult of official violence if it were not, nor could we begin to see war as a problem and something to be surpassed, something I have assumed as relatively uncontentious from the outset. Yet, because war is politically, economically, and above all, conceptually *situated*, it must be recognised not as primarily a moral, but a *political* problem. Since the Vietnam War, resistance to war has been fundamentally based on revulsion at its violence and destructiveness and the popular culture that naturalise it. This resistance has been primarily rhetorical and gestural, as it befits its interest in the aesthetics of war and in tune with the general aestheticisation of politics of the time. It has rested on general humanist clichés about community, fraternity and an ideal social future. In other words, it has relied on a banal and unsustainable understanding of the mutual alienation of the human and war. This conception is not wrong in any simple sense, but it is too uncomplicated to deal with the dynamics of the war/other complex, in which the human can be as much a justification for war as reason for scepticism towards it, and is indeed probably both. To engage with war properly, we have to realise that this kind of opposition is not enough. When war is in play, so is something else, war's various others. Humanist sentimentality often attempts to present what we have identified as war's others as unquestionable or non-negotiable: How can we possibly contest the value implicit in love, or sociality or human rights? Is not this the worst kind of post-modern relativism, in which we allow what should be absolute values to be held up for debate? Yet it is these various "values" that accompany and facilitate the emergence of war, and that always wrong-foot us when we attempt to reject it. Do we not want dictators to be removed, women's rights restored and ethnic cleansing resisted? If we are in favour of these goals, how can we resist the wars that aim to achieve them? Does not this make the rejection of war merely automatic and adolescent?

The refusal to debate these values results in both an impotent and unworldly rejection of war, on the one hand, and a mindless acquiescence to it, on the other. The argument of this book has been that it is necessary to understand the complexity of the implication of such values in war. This understanding requires the courage to rethink these values and the political will to engage unsentimentally with their historical function. Questioning war must involve a questioning of the very things in the name of which wars are fought, not in order simply to reject them, but to engage properly with their real historical and political function. If you are unwilling to deal with this dynamic and seek mere recourse to absolute rejections of war, or absolute endorsement of the values that oppose (and/or allow) war, then you risk remaining stuck in the cycle from which politics should always be attempting to free us. Just because they have failed us and have proven corrupt, easily intimidated and willingly compromised, we should not exempt parliaments from being one place amongst others where such politics should take place. In short, wherever it happens, the politics of war must also provide a properly critical account of war's other.

Our inherited models of politics have opted either for the grand narrative approach to the realisation of optimal ideological goals or else a molecularism, in which social fractions either withstand or disrupt the forces attempting to limit them. The first relies on a model of a uniform and collective trajectory of human development, which can no longer be sustained, as well as having a weak understanding of what Foucault so ably identified as the "regional" (Foucault, 2003, p. 27) way in which power operates. The second fails to produce more general insight into the dynamics of human collectivity, the politics of the economic in particular. The pitting of these two models of politics against one another defined post-modern debate. Yet, we may be now confronting a political epoch in which neither of these ways of thinking about politics helps us: the first because it aims to recover an older sense of human universality that is long gone, irrecoverable, ineffective and probably already unlamented; the second because the radical disruption of identity and administration, however relevant it remains to challenging the silent violence of culture, policy and social institutions, will not reassemble the sites of collective intention, scrutiny and negotiation that we will need in order to deal with the challenges of the politics of climate change—economic activity discovering its final limits, the resulting dislocation of human populations inequitably experienced, the threat of states acting unilaterally to secure their interests regardless of the consequences and so on. What we will be confronting will be a series of situations that will not be easily assimilable to theoretical models developed in wholly different contexts, co-ordinated as they were, first, with the expansion and, then, the contraction of Western historicity. This future could well produce a set of unfolding or overlapping crises in which wars develop. It will be absolutely crucial to understand the dynamic behind these wars: What are they being fought for? It may be true that globalisation will not result in the liquidation of the nation state, as Hirst and others have argued. Yet, in the twenty-first century, however pragmatically persistent the nation state may be, it lacks any enduring sense of natural inevitability, and contests with economic, religious and ethnic allegiances which may co-ordinate with it—from the potentially unknowable flows of capital through an increasingly abstract financial market to the bonds of fundamentalist dogmatism— but which may overwhelm it as well. There is and will continue to be a remaking of the plural relationships that will cluster around a set of unrecognisable warfares. War will not perhaps be the instrument of established social collectivities or an expression of their values, but the thing that brings them into existence in the first place, inventing ideological and dogmatic formations hitherto unknown, or loose coalitions of established national and international institutions. Who will fight which wars in the name of what? As we have seen, what gives rise to a war, what justifies it can also define the very point of view from which it can be resisted, not that our attitude to war should always and everywhere be simply one of refusal. Economic security, political rights and even peace are examples of the double constructs in the name of which war can be both defended and critiqued.

My argument is that, given the unpredictability of our political future and the superannuation of the political models we have inherited, a theoretical construct like the war/other complex may provide one way in which future situations may be thought not ideologically but pragmatically. Traditionally war has been treated as if it is a discrete event, anticipated by causes and followed by consequences, but a singular thing nevertheless. The war/other complex allows us to see war in its embeddedness in the unfolding of global social relations in general. In this way, it may not only provide a more pragmatic way of understanding a future politics, but by reinventing new ways of imagining the collective and the specific dynamic by which it may subsume individual bodies and events, it may take over the function of our previous political paradigms.

Whenever the West is attacked it always believes that it is the Enlightenment that is the target. The Enlightenment legacy is still clung to as if it is novel and threatening to other societies, still insurgent, fragile, ever uncompromised and futuristic. Soldiers are sent out to defend or expand this legacy, or simply just to demonstrate that it cannot be intimidated, and will be defended. These soldiers execute saturation bombings, high-tech sweeps of civilian neighbourhoods and brutal displays of the range of their matériel. They believe in the enlightened righteousness of the massive show of force. Soon, they will disrupt social networks, disable economic life, ridicule culture and perhaps even torture detainees and rape children. The havoc they wreak will be far more destructive than the regimes they have replaced. But this will not really matter or it will be dismissed as accidental, because they are agents of the Enlightenment, whose eventual triumph will justify everything. In conquered territory, political institutions will probably only be established via weak coalitions of communal groups or through the co-operation of warlords. In this way, a country can settle into a loose if pessimistic quiet, and you may even be able to pretend that the most sensational or publicised of your enemies, the Viet Cong or Al-Qaida, for example, have been defeated. At home, in pursuit of this defence of the Enlightenment, police powers will be increased, the courts will be restrained and the media either seduced or intimidated. Yet this war will provoke ever greater activism on behalf of human rights and the Enlightenment legacy. Lawyers, judges, politicians, journalists, Internet bloggers, new political movements and even the leader writers of broadsheet newspapers will reassert their commitment to freedom and democracy.

The relationship between war and human rights has never been any less complicated than this. Human rights achieved their present prominence not through ideological deliberation, but as the principles which victors, hoping for a new international covenant, held up as what they had been fighting for in the Second World War. Delivered by war, clear commitments to human rights would help both to prevent wars and also, ironically, to decide which ones to fight. Derrida said famously that there is no law without force (Derrida, 2002). There is no law without at least the possibility of it needing, one day, to be enforced. Analogously, there are no human rights without the possibility that they might one day have to be fought for. The history and politics of human rights in our era are thoroughly caught up in war. Human rights are simultaneously what wars have produced, what wars are for and how we can resist them. There are no human rights without the possibility of war and vice versa.

In post-modern society, a commitment to human rights became a substitute for political engagement. Politics was so compromised, it seemed useless and immovable. Yet, the fact that the historical function of doctrines of human rights is implicated inextricably in warfare shows that there can be no separation of human rights activism from the most brutal execution of physical power. This is not to say that the two are identical. Nor is it to reduce the importance of the clash between them: human rights and violence may be historically connected but they remain in fierce tension, even in contradiction with one another. This is the exact problem that we need to confront: we have an almost automatic ethical obligation to reduce violence, yet we cannot ignore the fact that simple goodwill cannot ensure rights. On the other hand, violence implicitly violates: mutilating bodies, casting lives adrift, ruining social networks, obliterating cultures and compromising the freedom of civic identities. There is no outside of the relationship between human rights and power, because there is no war simply and resolutely separable from its other. Human rights are a political and not a moral issue therefore, and our hopes of advancing them requires a renewal of, and commitment to, the political relationship.

Bibliography

Badiou, Alain (2006) *Polemics*, trans. Steve Corcoran. London: Verso.
Bataille, Georges (1986) *Erotism: Death and Sensuality*, trans. Mary Dalwood. San Francisco: City Lights Books.
—— (1989) *Theory of Religion*, trans. Robert Hurley. New York: Zone Books.
—— (1991) *The Accursed Share: An Essay on General Economy Volume One*, trans. Robert Hurley. New York: Zone Books.
Baudrillard, Jean (1995) *The Gulf War Did Not Take Place*, trans. Paul Patton. Bloomington: Indiana University Press.
—— (2002) *The Spirit of Terrorism and Other Essays*, trans. Chris Turner. London: Verso.
Bauman, Zygmunt (2001) "Wars of the Globalisation Era," *European Journal of Social Theory*, 4(1), 11–28.
Beardsworth, Richard (1996) *Derrida & the Political*, London: Routledge.
Bennington, Geoffrey (1994) *Legislations: The Politics of Deconstruction*, London: Verso.
Blood, Susan (2002) "The Poetics of Expenditure," *MLN*, 117(4), 836–857.
Borradori, Giovanna (2003) *Philosophy in a Time of Terror: Dialogues with Jürgen Habermas and Jacques Derrida*, Chicago: University of Chicago Press.
Botting, Fred and Scott Wilson (1998) *Bataille: A Critical Reader*, Oxford: Blackwell.
Bourke, Joanna (2000) *An Intimate History of Killing: Face-to-face Killing in Twentieth Century Warfare*, London: Granta.
Buonamano, Roberto (1998) "The Economy of Violence: Derrida on Law and Justice," *Ratio Juris*, 11(2), 168–79.
Butler, Judith (2004) *Precarious Life: The Powers of Mourning and Violence*, London: Verso.
Christopher, Paul (2004) *The Ethics of War and Peace: An Introduction to Legal and Moral Issues*, Upper Saddle River, NJ: Pearson Prentice-Hall.
Clausewitz, Carl von (1968) *On War*, trans. J. J. Graham. London: Penguin Books.
Critchley, Simon (1999a) *The Ethics of Deconstruction: Derrida and Levinas*. 2nd edn, Edinburgh: Edinburgh University Press.
—— (1999b) *Ethics—Politics—Subjectivity: Essays on Derrida, Levinas and Contemporary French Thought*, London: Verso.
Deleuze, Gilles and Felix Guattari (1987) *A Thousand Plateaus: Capitalism and Schizophrenia, Volume 2*, trans. Brian Massumi. Minneapolis: University of Minnesota Press.
—— (1994) *What is Philosophy?* trans. Graham Burchell and Hugh Tomlinson. London: Verso.
De Landa, Manuel (1991) *War in the Age of Intelligent Machines*, New York: Zone Books.
Der Derian, James (2001) *Virtuous War: Mapping the Military-Industrial-Media-Entertainment Complex*, London: Routledge.

Derrida, Jacques (1994) *Specters of Marx: The State of the Debt, the Work of Mourning & the New International*, trans. Peggy Kamuf. New York and London: Routledge.
—— (1997) *Politics of Friendship*, trans. George Collins. London: Verso.
—— (1999) *Adieu to Emmanuel Levinas*, trans. Pascale-Anne Brault and Michael Naas. Stanford: Stanford University Press.
—— (2002) "Force of Law: 'The Mystical Foundations of Authority'" in *Acts of Religion*, ed. Gil Anidjar, trans. Mary Quaintance and Gil Anidjar. London and New York: Routledge.
—— (2005) *Rogues: Two Essays on Reason*, trans. Pascale-Anne Brault and Michael Naas. Stanford: Stanford University Press.
Dinstein, Yoram (2004) *War, Aggression and Self-Defense*, Cambridge: Cambridge University Press.
Douzinas, Costas (2000) *The End of Human Rights: Critical Legal Thought at the Turn of the Century*, Oxford: Hart.
Flathman, Richard E. (2002) *Thomas Hobbes: Skepticism, Individuality and Chastened Politics*, Lanham MD: Rowman & Littlefield.
Foucault, Michel (2003) *Society Must be Defended*, trans. David Macey. London: Allen Lane.
Freud, Sigmund (1984) *On Metapsychology*, ed. Angela Richards, trans. James Strachey. London: Penguin Books.
—— (1985) *Civilization, Society and Religion*, ed. Angela Richards, trans. James Strachey. London: Penguin Books.
Hardt, Michael and Antonio Negri (2004) *Multitude: War and Democracy in the Age of Empire*, London: Penguin Books.
Hendrickson, Ryan C. (2002) *The Clinton Wars: The Constitution, Congress and War Powers*, Vanderbilt UP: Nashville.
Hirst, Paul (2005) *Space and Power: Politics, War and Architecture*, Cambridge: Polity.
Hobbes, Thomas (1996) *Leviathan*, ed. J. C. A. Gaskin. Oxford: Oxford University Press.
Hoskins, Andrew (2004) *Televising War: From Vietnam to Iraq*, London: Continuum.
Kant, Immanuel (1957) *Perpetual Peace*, ed. Lewis White Beck. Indianapolis: Liberal Arts Press.
Kellner, Douglas (2000) "Virilio, War and Technology: Some Critical Reflections," in *Paul Virilio: From Modernism to Hypermodernism and Beyond*, ed. John Armitage. London: Sage.
Kolko, Gabriel (1995) *Century of War: Politics, Conflicts and Society Since 1914*, New York: New Press.
Land, Nick (1992) *The Thirst for Annihilation*, London: Routledge.
Levinas, Emmanuel (1969) *Totality and Infinity: An Essay on Exteriority*, trans. Alphonso Lingis. Pittsburgh: Duquesne University Press.
Llewelyn, John (2002) *Appositions of Jacques Derrida and Emmanuel Levinas*, Bloomington: Indiana University Press.
Mbembe, Achille (2003) "Necropolitics," *Public Culture*, 15(1), 11–40.
Money-Kyrle, Roger (1951) *Psychoanalysis and Politics, a Contribution to the Psychology of Politics and Morals*, London: Duckworth.
Moskos, Charles C., John Allen Williams and David R. Segal (eds). *The Postmodern Miltary: Armed Forces After the Cold War*, Oxford: Oxford University Press.
Münkler, Herfried (2005) *The New Wars*, trans. Patrick Camiller, Cambridge: Polity.

Neiberg, Michael (2001) *Warfare in World History*, London: Routledge.
Noys, Benjamin (2000) *Georges Bataille*, London: Pluto Press.
O'Donovan, Oliver (2003) *The Just War Revisited*, Cambridge: Cambridge University Press.
Rodin, David (2002) *War and Self-Defense*, Oxford: Clarendon Press.
Rose, Jacqueline (1993) *Why War?—Psychoanalysis, Politics and the Return to Melanie Klein*, Oxford: Oxford University Press.
Schmitt, Carl (1996) *The Concept of the Political*, trans. George Schwab. Chicago: University of Chicago Press.
—— (2007) *Theory of the Partisan*, trans. G. L. Ulmen. New York: Telos Press.
Shaw, Martin (2005) *The New Western Way of War*, London: Polity.
Theweleit, Klaus (1987) *Male Fantasies, Volume 1: Women, Floods, Bodies, History*, trans. Stephen Conway. Cambridge: Polity Press.
—— (1989) *Male Fantasies Volume 2: Male Bodies: Psychoanalysing the White Terror*, trans. Chris Turner and Erika Carter. Cambridge: Polity Press.
Thomson, A. J. P. (2005) *Deconstruction and Democracy: Derrida's Politics of Friendship*, London: Continuum.
Tritle, Lawrence A. (2000) *From Melos to My Lai: War and Survival*, London: Routledge.
Virilio, Paul (1986) *Speed and Politics: An Essay on Dromology*, trans. Mark Polizotti. New York: Semiotext(e).
—— (1989) *War and Cinema: The Logistics of Perception*, trans. Patrick Camiller. London: Verso.
—— (2000) *The Information Bomb*, trans. Chris Turner. London: Verso.
—— (2002) *Ground Zero*, trans. Chris Turner. London: Verso.
Virilio, Paul and Sylvère Lotringer (1983) *Pure War*, trans. Mark Polizotti. New York: Semiotext(e).
Walzer, Michael (2004) *Arguing About War*, New Haven: Yale University Press.
Žižek, Slavoj (2002) *Welcome to the Desert of the Real: Five Essays on 11th September and Related Dates*, London: Verso.

Index

Abu Ghraib, 109
Afghanistan, 79, 133, 147, 152
Africa, 152
Agamben, Giorgio, 79, 128, 148, 160
aggression, 40
   Freud on, 49–58, 60–2
Al-Qaida, 79, 156
apartheid, 151
army, the, 51, 54–5
art, 82
Artaud, Antonin, 91
atrocity, 52, 56, 60, 77, 85, 86, 96, 113, 157
Auschwitz, 136
Australia, 111
Aztecs, the, 69–70

Badiou, Alain, 155–7, 161
   on the war/revolution dialectic, 156–7
Balkans War, 109, 142
Bataille, Georges, 5, 63–82, 84–8, 90, 99, 105
   The Accursed Share, 64–70
   on restricted and general economies, 64–9, 72, 76, 77, 78
   Theory of Religion, 70–7
Baudrillard, Jean, 144–8, 157, 162
Bauman, Zygmunt, 141–4
Blair, Tony, 6
Bonaparte, Napoleon, 30, 37

capitalism, 95, 142, 166
Christianity, 111–12
cinema, 132
civil war, 15
civilisation, 45–50, 58, 59, 61, 62
Clausewitz, Carl von, 4, 5, 9, 105, 119, 120, 137–9, 149
   on "ideal war", 29
   on the military genius, 30–4, 36, 38, 39
   On War, 28–38

climate change, 166
Clinton presidency, 163
Cold War, 96, 130, 133, 136, 137, 141, 144, 162
colonialism, 151–2
commonwealth, 10–11, 13, 15, 18, 19, 21
communism, 164
consumption, 65, 67, 71, 80–1

death, 42, 47, 56, 57
   death instinct, 57, 60–2
declaration of war, 2
Deleuze, Gilles and Felix Guattari, 5, 77, 81, 82–98, 105, 152
   on affect, 87
   on nomadism, 82–6, 91, 92
   "Treatise on Nomadology", 82–98
   What is Philosophy?, 86
democracy, 80, 103, 111, 148, 149, 163, 164
Derrida, Jacques, 1, 2, 5, 40, 86, 98–117, 130, 151, 157, 161, 168
   "Force of Law", 79
   on the friend/enemy distinction, 105–12, 99, 115, 158
   on negotiation, 99, 114
   Philosophy in a Time of Terror, 1
   on responsibility, 100
   Rogues, 79
   Specters of Marx, 111
desire, 11–19, 21
difference, 43, 48
diplomacy, 31
Dumézil, Georges, 82
duty, 20, 21, 23

ego, 44, 45, 52–7
Einstein, Albert, 59–60
Eisenhower, Dwight D., 134
enlightenment, 167–8
entertainment, 97–8

Eros, 44, 56, 58
ethics, 20, 21–4
excess, 65–8, 76–8, 86, 98

fear, 12
Foucault, Michel, 29, 137, 162, 164
  on biopower, 126–9, 148
  on disciplinary power, 123–4, 127
  Society Must be Defended, 120–30
French Revolution, 37
Freud, Sigmund, 4, 40–63, 76, 88, 96, 105, 130, 162
  on ambivalence, 4, 40, 44, 47, 52, 55, 62
  "Beyond the Pleasure Principle", 57, 60–1
  Civilisation and Its Discontents, 49–50, 52–9
  "Group Psychology and the Analysis of the Ego", 50–2
  on leaders, 50–2, 54–6, 62
  on the primal father, 51, 54, 62
  "Thoughts for the Times on War and Death", 41–8
  Totem and Taboo, 47, 54
Fukuyama, Francis, 111

globalisation, 141–4, 153
Guattari, Felix, *see* Deleuze
Guerrilla warfare, 94
Gulf War, 144–8, 157, 162

Hardt, Michael and Antonio Negri, 148–50
Hiroshima, 136
Hirst, Paul, 139–41, 144, 166
history, 125–6
Hobbes, Thomas, 4, 9–19, 20, 21, 23, 28, 38, 40, 46, 62, 100, 120, 158, 161, 162, 163
  Leviathan, 9–19, 123
Hollywood, 158
Holocaust, 162
hospitality, 103
human rights, 6, 7, 111–13, 149, 160, 161–8
Hussein, Saddam, 79–80

identity, 40, 98, 102
indigenous people, 111
individual, 17–19, 72–6, 84, 85, 91, 103, 110, 121, 128
industrial war, 66
Inquisition, the, 60
International Criminal Court, 81
Iraq, 79–80, 113, 147, 149, 152
Islam, 108, 139, 147
Israel, 154

Just War theory, 149

Kant, Immanuel, 4, 19–28, 62, 103, 117, 128, 162
  Perpetual Peace, 19–28

Lacan, Jacques, 158
law, 103
  Kant on, 22–7, 124, 126, 128
Levinas, Emmanuel, 22, 98, 99, 100–5
liberty, 18
life, 19
love, 47–9, 51, 53–6, 59, 60, 62

Mao Zedong, 156
Mbembe, Achille, 151–2, 154, 161
metaphysics, 98
military society, 69, 76–8, 83, 85, 88, 90, 94, 95, 96
morality, 11, 19
  Freud on, 51
Münkler, Herfried, 137, 152–5, 161
Mutually Assured Destruction, 96, 130, 162

narcissism, 56–8
nature, 9, 58, 61, 71
  Hobbes on, 10–19
  Kant on, 22–7
Nazism, 151, 164
Negri, Antonio, *see* Hardt, Michael
New World Order, 145
Nietzsche, Friedrich, 99

Ottoman Empire, 109

Palestine, 154
Patriot Act, 103

peace, 11, 15, 16, 20, 22–8, 61, 62, 99–105, 108, 116, 120, 135, 149, 151, 154
Petrarch, 121
politics, 20, 22, 28, 31, 116, 130, 134, 141, 161
power, 12, 120–4
primitive people, 33, 43, 47, 49, 50, 88
psychoanalysis, 40–2, 44, 47–9, 62, 157

racism, 126–9
rape, 154, 157
reason, 20, 23, 27, 36
    practical reason, 21, 22, 26
religion, 70–7, 85
repression, 44–6, 48, 63
Revolution in Military Affairs, 157
Rose, Jacqueline, 48–9

sacrifice, 69, 71, 73–4, 76
sadism, 57
Schmitt, Carl, 79, 98, 99, 100, 105–12, 114
science, Freud on, 41–2, 59
September 11, 2001, 79, 142, 157, 158–61
social policy treated as war, 2, 3, 80, 116, 149, 153, 154, 163
sovereignty, 4, 21, 78, 82, 83, 89, 120–9, 151–2, 158
    Hobbes on, 9–11, 15–19
Soviet Union, 133
space, 94, 139–41
State, the, 27, 43, 45, 110, 114, 116, 140–2, 153, 166
    Deleuze and Guattari on, 82–98

subjectivity, 11, 80, 142
    Bataille on, 63, 72–3, 78, 79
    Deleuze and Guattari on, 87, 90
    Foucault on, 121–4, 128
    Freud on, 40–63
    Levinas on, 101, 103
Sun Tzu, 135
superego, 52–4

technology, 134–5, 138
terrorism, 1, 79–82, 154
Thanatos, 59, 61, 62
Thirty Years War, 153
time, 15, 135
Total War, 95–6, 136, 138
Treaty of Lausanne, 109
Treaty of Westphalia, 142, 148

United States, 79–82, 136, 155, 158, 160

Vietnam War, 133, 164
violence, 46, 47, 48, 51, 52, 59, 68, 72–4, 76, 77, 80, 83, 90, 97, 114, 122, 146, 153, 154, 158
Virilio, Paul, 130–8, 145
    The Information Bomb, 136–7
    on logistics, 130, 132–6
    Pure War, 133–6
    on speed, 132–3
    Speed and Politics, 130–3

warrior society, 69, 76–8, 83, 88
war on terror, 3, 96, 116, 141, 145, 147, 149, 151, 153, 156, 162
World War One, 40–5, 56, 67, 132, 136
World War Two, 67, 155, 168

Žižek, Slavoj, 157–61, 162